Advance Praise for *Problem Solver*

"*Problem Solver* is not just a book about how to make better decisions. It's a pathway to deeper self-knowledge. Discovering how we decide sheds light on the mystery of our cognition—what we listen for, what we credit, and what we dismiss. Understanding our hidden tendencies and biases is essential to living a more examined and rewarding life."
—**David Bornstein, *New York Times* columnist; CEO, Solutions Journalism Network**

"*Problem Solver* gets us focused on the one big skill that unlocks all the rest; the one self-assessment that sets the stage for every other choice we make about who we are and how we show up in the world; the one lens that sharpens our focus on every situation we face, no matter how challenging. It's impossible to read this and not feel like you're discovering something absolutely core to your happiness and success in life."
—**Andrew Mangino, Cofounder and CEO, the Future Project**

"A revolutionary way of communicating. Until I read this book, I never considered that we all listen differently and that by understanding each archetype's biases, I could learn to be a better communicator. It has changed the way I approach conversation."
—**Van Hutcherson, Managing Director, Jones Trading**

"*Problem Solver* is two tools in one. First, its framework of decision-making processes helps you understand, and thereby address, the blind spots in your process. Second, as shown through examples in the book, by applying the framework to peers' processes (personal or professional), you can more effectively communicate by providing information in the way they process it, thereby coming to better decisions."
—**Joshua Musher, Chief Operating Officer, *Arbiter Partners Capital Management***

"*Problem Solver* helps us understand that who we are is a series of choices and that improving our decision-making can improve the quality of our lives."
—Liz Landau, CFP and Owner, Landau Advisory LLC

"Cheryl Strauss Einhorn's *Problem Solver* allows each individual to develop a personal and customized framework for making better decisions. You will learn how to gather the most relevant pieces of information and squeeze out maximum benefit. Consequently, in any decision-making setting, you will be able to minimize the adverse effects of common cognitive biases and fully exploit your strengths. And during this process, you may even be able to answer the question: Who am I?"
—Alok Kumar, Miami Herbert Business School, University of Miami

"In *Problem Solver*, Einhorn demystifies the act of decision-making with a practical and engaging set of tools that help decode the reader's personal style and approach to working with others. Whether you are an experienced leader or just want to strengthen interpersonal relationships, this book is a terrific compass on your journey."
—Eric Dawson, CEO, Rivet; Cofounder, Peace First

PROBLEM SOLVER

PROBLEM SOLVER

Maximizing Your Strengths to Make

Better Decisions

CHERYL STRAUSS EINHORN

An AREA Method Book

Published in association with Cornell University Press
Ithaca and London

First published 2023 in association with Cornell University Press

Library of Congress Cataloging-in-Publication Data

Names: Einhorn, Cheryl Strauss, author.
Title: Problem solver : maximizing your strengths to make better decisions / Cheryl Strauss Einhorn.
Description: Ithaca : Cornell University Press, 2023. | "An AREA Method book." | Includes bibliographical references.
Identifiers: LCCN 2022032443 (print) | LCCN 2022032444 (ebook) | ISBN 9781501768002 (hardcover) | ISBN 9781501768033 (paperback) | ISBN 9781501768019 (epub) | ISBN 9781501768026 (pdf)
Subjects: LCSH: Decision making. | Problem solving.
Classification: LCC BF448 .E36 2023 (print) | LCC BF448 (ebook) | DDC 153.8/3—dc23/eng/20220919
LC record available at https://lccn.loc.gov/2022032443
LC ebook record available at https://lccn.loc.gov/2022032444

Have you ever sold anything door-to-door? As I was wrapping up the first draft of this book, my nineteen-year-old son, Mitchell, was doing just that. He was selling educational textbooks here in the United States, but far from home in a rural, low-income community where he felt very much an outsider. One morning he approached a house with an empty driveway and rang the bell. There was no answer. Later that afternoon he dropped by the same house, now with three cars in the driveway. He rang the bell again; still no answer. Dogged in his pursuit of business, when he finished for the evening about 9:00 p.m., he swung by the house one more time. There were nine cars in front. This time, when he rang the bell, a man in his fifties answered and asked, "What can I do for you?"

My son looked down the driveway at the nine cars and looked back at this tired-looking man. There was one thing he really didn't need: a car. But how do you break the ice to talk about something that perhaps this man, or his family, did need? Gesturing at the vehicles in the driveway, my son answered. "I'm here to sell you a car."

The man was stunned only for a beat before they shared a hearty laugh.

My son had collected information not from a book, or a set of data per se, but directly from the world he saw in front of him, and he used it to introduce himself, not who *he* was but rather what he'd noticed.

This book is dedicated to my son and to everyone who wants to approach decisions in a way that better connects them with others and the world around them.

A new type of thinking is essential if mankind is to survive and move toward higher levels.

—Albert Einstein

Contents

Acknowledgments

A few years ago, I gave a TED talk titled *When Your Inner Voice Lies to You*, about how we lead ourselves astray by seeing the world not as it is but as we are. I talked about how our inner voice, which we see as our "true" voice, often functions instead as a dirty windshield, seeing the world clouded by false assumptions, misremembering, and cognitive biases. What's more, we don't recognize that it's happening.

The good news is that we can wake ourselves up to how cognitive biases get in our way. From there we can learn to transform the texture of how we engage with the world to improve it and our relationships.

As the great novelist James Baldwin once observed, "Nothing is fixed, forever and forever and forever. . . . We made the world we are living in and we have to make it over."[1]

Waking ourselves up so that we can make the world over is, at its heart, the exploration of this book: to more completely inspect the personal psychology of our decision-making—the data of our lives. In so doing, we can identify how to "make over" the world we live in with purposeful action that alters our reality in some subtle but meaningful way so that we make our big decisions better—and make them together, with the people who matter to us.

I had a lot of good help on this journey. I benefited from conversations and thoughtful feedback from numerous people who were instrumental in discussing and working on the concepts and writing of this book. As philosopher Hannah Arendt observed, "The smallest act in the most limited circumstances bears the seed of . . . boundlessness, because one deed, and sometimes one word, suffices to change every constellation."[2]

To my colleague at Decisive and dear friend Emma Trout, you will always be, in my eyes, a true Dream Director to me, even if it was a title you held long ago. You continue to translate the passion and purpose of our work into action every day. To Cathleen Barnhart, who once taught my kids and now has taught me not only about storytelling and writing but also about friendship, this book would not have been a reality without your thoughtful advice, encouragement, expertise, and editing.

I also want to thank Peter Lawrence, a former student, later a friend and coteacher with me at Columbia Business School. To my parents, who were close readers and cheerleaders, to Dean Smith, the director of Duke University Press, who believed in me, my AREA Method, and this book: thank you for your continued guidance and your sharp eye. Many other friends and colleagues read the manuscript and shared their thoughtful, useful feedback: Vadim Axelrod, Tony Blair, David Bornstein, Kevin Carmody, Liz Landau, Andrew Mangino, Josh Musher, and my team at Cornell University Press led by Mahinder Kingra; saying thank you cannot convey my true thanks.

Thank you as well to readers across the globe who have reached out and connected with me through my website to share their lives and their big decisions over the years; your stories inspire me.

And to Ari and Tim, whose real identities I have hidden in order to protect the important work you're doing, thank you for letting me follow your journey and support you in your mission. You truly live author and Anglican priest Nicky Gumbel's credo, "Let your dreams be bigger than your fears, your actions louder than your words and your faith stronger than your feelings."[3]

With gratitude and appreciation,
Cheryl

This chart, which you will meet again in chapter 8, is a snapshot synopsis of the different ways in which people tend to approach problem-solving. All of us approach problem-solving with a set of skills—and a set of habits and biases. In my work on decision-making, I've identified five different decision-making archetypes, which appear below. This book is intended to help you identify your archetype—your Problem Solver Profile—so that you can make big decisions better and work more effectively with the other decision-makers in your life.

CHEETAH SHEET 1
Problem Solver Profiles

This chart provides you with a synopsis of the different ways that people tend to approach problem-solving. Refer to this chart to better understand your own approach or to consider the decision-making approaches of others. Cheetah Sheet 6: PSP Strengths and Blind Spots will expand on these PSP characteristics.

ARCHETYPES	STRENGTHS	BLIND SPOTS
Adventurer	Confidence Speed Efficiency	Optimism bias Planning bias Confirmation bias Closeness-communication bias
Detective	Committed to facts Rational Realistic	Confirmation bias Planning fallacy Projection bias Frame blindness
Listener	Trusting Relational Supportive	Authority bias Liking bias Narrative bias Social proof bias
Thinker	Thoroughness Thoughtfulness Caution	Loss aversion Relativity bias Authority bias Frame blindness
Visionary	Imaginative Innovative Individualistic	Optimism bias Saliency bias Scarcity bias Planning fallacy

PROBLEM SOLVER

Introduction: The Data of Living

Learning without thought is labor lost.
—Confucius

When we think about the future, we hope for many of the same things: good health for ourselves and our families, a secure income, a basic sense of safety, and control over our lives. In these uncertain times, even such simple desires can seem out of reach because the future feels so unpredictable. But the future has always been unpredictable, unruly, and beyond our knowledge.

Still, there are skills and tools that we all can use to plan for our future that are practical, actionable, and available to everyone. These skills bake our values and desires into our plans so that we can better work toward our particular vision of the future. Like all skills, these planning and decision-making tools require both an investment of time and a willingness to try new ways of thinking.

But isn't that investment worth it?

Ironically, decision-making is generally not even seen as a skill that we might want to develop, especially when we consider the universality of its application. All of us make decisions every day, large and small. Who we are is a series of choices, and our decisions are the data of living.

Rarely, though, do we take the time to examine our decisions or even look inward to consider the psychology of our decision-making. *How do we, personally, identify and understand our decision-making approach and its implications?*

Although there are some decision-making tools available (including my books about personal and professional problem-solving, *Problem Solved* and *Investing in Financial Research*), the existing tools and strategies don't guide us to learn about ourselves. Instead they generally treat us as if we are all the same. However, any set of tools or strategies will resonate differently with different people because the values behind our decisions are deeply personal, and our decision-making tendencies are a reflection of that individuality.

Whether we turn to a decision-making tree or make a decision from instinct, there are several misunderstandings that can trip us up:

1. We tend to rely on the same types of information for making decisions without recognizing that there may be other, and sometimes more, useful kinds of information out there.
2. We often assume that there is a neutral "right answer," and that our own values and desires should not be part of the process.
3. We rely on well-worn pathways of thinking and making decisions that may—but equally may not—have served us well in the past.

We also may feel that we can't slow down to truly examine the decision we're about to make. We have emails to get through, kids to pick up at soccer practice, and a quick trip we must make to the supermarket (the dog's bath can wait until tomorrow). And if we do think about slowing down: Why slow down to sit in discomfort? Isn't it so much nicer to get the decision out of the way and then sit down with a fine glass of chardonnay?

But taking the time to cultivate curiosity—about yourself, your habits, your values, and the decision-making strategies of others—may alleviate regret later. Investing time now to learn first about who you are as a decision maker, second about who others are, and third about how you can more confidently make decisions will, in the long term, speed up and improve your decision-making efficacy and dynamism for a good cause: your satisfying future.

In *Problem Solver* you will learn:

1. Your Problem Solver Profile (PSP): your personal approach to decision-making
2. Other Problem Solver Profiles, the different kinds of decision-making archetypes, their strengths and potential blind spots

3. How different decision-making approaches impact how we think about, assess, and analyze risk
4. Cognitive biases as they interact with and pertain to Problem Solver Profiles (biases that work on each of us individually and that impact relationships: decision-making is not siloed so we need to address both always)
5. How to use Problem Solver Profiles to distinguish ambiguity from uncertainty
6. How to bolster your decision-making strengths and limit your potential blind spots
7. How Problem Solver Profiles interact differently with data
8. How to discern situationality and become a dynamic decision maker
9. How your Problem Solver Profile impacts your outlook on life

By the end of this book, you won't just look out into a future, you'll be equipped to move forward into *your* future with confidence.

To Know Thyself: How to Use This Book

The beginning of all wisdom is wonder.
—Aristotle

Before we dive deeper into the process of decision-making and your specific strengths and blind spots as a decision maker, a note about how to use this book. Throughout the book you'll find a series of strategic stops with a graphic organizer to aid your work and thinking. These worksheets, called Cheetah Sheets, are named after the cheetah, the fastest land animal whose hunting skills come not from acceleration alone, which can reach up to almost sixty miles an hour in three strides, but instead from the animal's unique ability to *decelerate* quickly—slowing down by as much as nine miles an hour *in a single stride*. That deceleration is more powerful than simply revving like a race car because it allows the cheetah to make the tight turns that give it an advantage over its fast and nimble prey. The animal's ability to decelerate provides flexibility and maneuverability in the hunt; should the cheetah pivot, change, or stay the course to reach its target?

Like the cheetah, the Cheetah Sheets in this book will offer strategic stops that guide you through a series of questions to prompt you to build and hone the skills that you need to harness your problem-solver knowledge to become a more agile and dynamic decision maker. Specifically, they will provide you with key questions that you will want to ask of yourself and the other stakeholders involved in your decisions and in the problems that you are solving. For many of the Cheetah Sheets, I also provide you with a filled-out example template so you can see how someone else answered the Cheetah Sheet questions. A full list of the Cheetah Sheets can be found in the table of contents.

The Cheetah Sheet list will also enable you to use this book like a workbook long after an initial read. By flipping to the sheets you want to use, you can check and challenge your biases, assumptions, and judgments and consider the incentives of other people with whom you make decisions.

Look at the different tools and charts I describe as suggestions and feel free to refine them however it feels best to you. But keep in mind: by pushing yourself out of your comfort zone with this book's resources, you will push your thinking in constructive ways, not only as the decision maker you are today but as the decision maker you want to become.

As a handy reference to keep track of the terminology and the many problem solvers that you'll meet in these pages, you'll find a glossary and a list of problem solvers, their PSPs, and their decisions in the appendix.

The Cheetah Sheets, which I introduced in my first book, *Problem Solved*, have worked for me, for the clients in my consulting and professional development work, and for countless students in my classrooms over the years. Here, they will help you break down the daunting task of controlling for and countering bias and working well with others to make decision-making into a more satisfying and manageable task.

To read more about how I've used Cheetah Sheets, my AREA Method decision-making system, and the decision-making archetypes that you'll learn about in this book, check out my website, blogs, podcasts, and case studies at areamethod.com.

Chapter One

How Do You Decide?

*You must learn a new way to think before you can master a new
way to be.*
–Marianne Williamson

The central Indian city of Ahmedabad is home to two and a half
million people. Located at the intersection of several road, rail, and air
routes, it has always been a center of trade. One of the goods being traded
in Ahmedabad: children.

Halfway around the world, in Washington State, Ari Patel had been
working for many years as a behavioral scientist for Costco. He was proud
of the work he was doing, studying human behavior and decision-making,
and he was one of the principal architects of the way customers navigate
through the company's retail warehouses to maximize sales.

Ari felt that he'd built a successful life for himself. However, a conversation with his godfather reminded him that he had always dreamed of
doing something very different: rescuing orphaned children living in poverty in India. Born in the United States to Indian parents, Ari had visited
the country when he was a small child, and he never forgot the destitution
and desperation he'd seen there. With his company's permission, he set
out straight from a company board meeting to travel to India, intent on
meeting with some of the children he wanted to help.

Arriving in New Delhi still in the rumpled suit he'd worn at the board
meeting, Ari walked from orphanage to orphanage, saying hello to the
orphans and asking about their stories. But at the end of the day, at a
local McDonald's, he met with a man who worked to rescue children

sold into sex slavery. The man described how very young girls were lined up, heavily made up, drugged and beaten, and sold like commodities. "When I heard about it," Ari recalls, "I snapped. I couldn't believe the horrors these children were subjected to." Ari didn't know exactly how he could make a difference; further, he had no experience working with children or working internationally, and he knew almost nothing about modern-day slavery. But he knew that he wanted to dedicate his life to stopping trafficking.

With his college roommate, Ari started Protect Her Life, a nonprofit organization dedicated to rescuing women and children stolen and sold into commercial sex work. But what did he know of India? Of how and why children and women became commercial sex workers? And what could he do to make a real difference?

Each problem seemed impossibly large and complicated. The first major decision Ari faced: Should he try to rescue women and children enslaved in sex trafficking, or should he try to disrupt the supply lines of victims by capturing the traffickers, which might also result in freeing the victims? And if he targeted the traffickers, whom should he target first? Would it make sense to arrest the trafficker who steals the most children, the one who is the most abusive to the children, the one who requires the children to service the most clients, or the one for whom documentation of wrongdoing could most likely lead to a conviction?

How could someone like Ari, with so little knowledge, background, or experience in the area he had suddenly decided to devote his life to, even begin to choose a path forward?

Ari was faced with a high-stakes decision, a decision that would have a long-term impact on the path forward for, and the success of, his nascent nonprofit—and on his own life. What was the impact he was looking for?

There are so many ways Ari could have answered his questions and moved forward with his decision-making and his nonprofit. The answers Ari found, and the path he chose to follow, ultimately worked for him and for his particular way of thinking about the future. But they might not work for you, in part because you too may have a decision-making style that mostly works for you. That's actually good news: for most complicated decisions there is no one right answer—but there is likely a right answer for Ari, as there is likely one for me, and one for you. They just might all be different.

How to find that "right answer" is, in part, a matter of four variables:

1. Identifying who you are as a decision maker,
2. Knowing what you value as a human being,
3. Appraising how well you work with the others involved in and affected by your decisions, and
4. Having an evidence-based process to research and vet your ideas that also thwarts biased thinking so that you can feel confident and have conviction in your path forward.

Knowing about yourself as a decision maker can help you understand how you approach problem-solving, your strengths, and potential pitfalls. This will help you understand why you come to certain conclusions and allow you to evaluate whether the conclusion may be valid or not. It will also better bring to light how you frame and work with risk, namely, what is your appetite for risk, how you assess it, and how you analyze it.

What you value as a human being can help you set the guardrails that guide your decision-making. They are the priorities that explain the "why." They can direct us toward a specific purpose, give us a sense of control by helping us discern when to say "yes," and, importantly, also reduce unhelpful rumination by making clear when to say "no" to a decision and pathway. The result: values provide both upside and downside protection. We know when we are getting closer to our goals and what can take us farther away from them.

Working well with other stakeholders involved in our decisions is the lynchpin that makes our decisions successful. For too long, decision-making has been approached as a solo endeavor. But we don't operate in a vacuum, and neither do our decisions.

To bring others along with us and give our decisions a holistic chance to succeed, we need to use an inclusive and fact-based process that allows us to effectively gather information, scrutinize its quality and meaning to us, and control for and counter the natural mental mistakes that we make due to unconscious bias.

Like many of us, Ari had never thought about how he approached his decisions. For Ari in particular, there was some irony to this as he'd spent his professional career analyzing how to influence other people's decision-making. So it was serendipity that just when he needed to look inward, he happened to land on the top of a small snowcapped mountain and bump into me.

I'd been invited to speak at a conference that took place in an octagonal building atop the summit of Powder Mountain, Utah. It was a sunny and clear winter day, and strong, warm sunlight poured through the floor-to-ceiling windows in the room as I talked with the audience about being more mindful and deliberate in high-stakes decision-making. I had just developed an app to help people identify what I was calling their Problem Solver Profile (PSP), the habits and patterns of behavior that drive our decision-making. My research and work on decision-making identified five different decision-making archetypes. Audience members began exploring the module, and the room got very quiet—for about fifteen minutes. At the point that the module began to reveal attendees' PSPs, the quiet was replaced by noisy, animated conversation.

At the end of my session, a young man—Ari—approached me, excited about the work we had done together and what he had learned about himself. He told me he was a Visionary, and he recognized that the profile "makes so much sense to me. It really explains a lot of things."

Ari was thrilled that his own sense of himself as a Visionary had been validated, particularly when he read that Visionaries are "drawn to exciting ideas" and can often get attached to "bold details"—his profile to a T. But Ari also saw himself in the weaknesses that are common blind spots for Visionaries. For example, the PSP module pointed out that Visionaries tend to lean on their imagination, and so they don't always do thorough research, racing toward their big ideas with limited, incomplete information.

Ari later told me, "Upon reading the Visionary description, I knew right away that I needed to talk with my mentors about taking things to completion and about how I could achieve a greater degree of structure and organization in my approach to work."

Like Ari, you too can experience the aha that he had when unlocking your strengths and potential pitfalls as a decision maker. The five Problem Solver Profiles that I had identified, and that I had shared with the conference attendees on that snowcapped mountain top, are Adventurers, Detectives, Listeners, Thinkers, and Visionaries. Adventurers tend to go with their gut reactions; Detectives like to follow the data; Listeners like to solicit the input of others; Thinkers like to identify multiple paths and outcomes; and Visionaries pride themselves on seeing pathways that others don't. Each archetype has significant strengths but also potential blind spots, a few key cognitive biases that may trip up a problem solver's ability to fully appraise a situation. And of course, many of us can be more than one type of problem solver, but in almost all cases there is one dominant approach that we lean on.

But we don't tend to think about how we make our decisions, we just make them—we go with our gut. Maybe that's because we never learned how or because we have so very many of them to make each and every day. Researchers tell us that we make up to forty thousand decisions in a day; Cornell University researchers recently concluded that we make over two hundred decisions each day *about food alone*. So it is surprising that until very recently schools didn't even think to teach us about decision-making—and most still don't—and we often don't discuss or learn explicitly about decision-making at home.

How could knowing about ourselves as decision makers impact, for example, the two-hundred-plus food-related decisions we make daily? What happens when you check into a hotel and are greeted with a fresh-from-the-oven chocolate chip cookie? If you're an Adventurer, who likes to make decisions quickly and instinctively, you'll likely grab the snack. But by recognizing that you tend to make decisions without caution—and that that's not always the best way to make decisions—you might more easily say no to the sweet snack sitting on the hotel lobby counter. If you're a Listener, who tends to heavily weigh others' opinions, you might hear those other voices and skip the cookie, especially if what you've been hearing is that you could shed a few pounds. But that may not be what *you* want—or even should—do. Understanding your Listener blind spots might help you learn to quiet those outside voices, better channel your own inner voice—and enjoy a delicious cookie!

The consequences of grabbing the sweet treat at the hotel check-in counter may be minimal, but to decide on your next car purchase—or which hospital to go to for surgery—with the same "go from the gut" attitude has much greater consequences.

In our lives we face many high-stakes decisions—ones where the outcome is unknown, the decision is likely to have a long-term impact on our lives, and the price for getting it wrong could be costly. Knowing more about our decision-making tendencies can be life-changing.

Do we want to do what we've done before? That's the basic question we face for almost every decision because that is how our minds operate, from the reel of our past experiences. It's all our mind knows, so it uses those memories to guide our future. Yet to answer that fundamental question about whether we want to repeat a prior decision requires several pieces of knowledge: How do we engage with our decisions? How have those decisions turned out? What can we do to make them better?

The truth is, our decisions are the only thing that we really have control over: *how* we choose matters. Yet we often end up with choices that are made by others, because we've—knowingly or unknowingly—abdicated the control over a decision. And frequently, we simply didn't notice that a decision is before us.

So why haven't we identified our decision-making style? We identify ourselves with all sorts of groups and categories—our race, our religion, our culture, our astrological sign, our geographical affiliation, the sports teams we root for, the hair-care products we swear by, the news we subscribe to (and the news we would never subscribe to!), yet we don't categorize what type of decision maker we are.

Many of the categories we choose as labels are predetermined for us by our families, our friends, and where we live. Our religious affiliation is often handed to us by our parents; the sports teams we root for are usually determined by where we live and who our friends root for. Likewise for the region we claim as home, whether we are southern or midwestern. So much of this identity formation happens when we are young, and we take it on and take pride in it without thinking about it—and that's not a bad thing. Our groups give us multiple ways to belong, and belonging is a basic human instinct.

Other kinds of categories, however, require us to be proactive and introspective—to study and analyze our own behavior and emotions. These kinds of group identities take time and effort to explore, whether they are about our passions, our politics, or our love language, and that exploration can be uncomfortable. But it's important work, work that can help us better realize our potential and live more satisfied lives. Schools and companies are just beginning to recognize the value of this foundational decision-making spadework and are doing it for a variety of reasons; it provides pathways to understanding and navigating learning differences, which can provide customized learning tools, professional development, and team building.

But often this introspection and analysis doesn't begin at home or in grade schools, in our foundational experiences, where we would benefit from being taught to think consciously about how we learn, how we form friendships, even how we give and receive love.

The idea that we don't necessarily share our decision-making approaches tends to dawn on us mostly over time—and without a manual for what to do with those differences or how to bridge them. By exploring the different Problem Solver Profiles and their implications, we can see that we often start our problem-solving from different entry points than others and that we value different aspects of the process. This new awareness can provide us with a more open mindset to make decisions that foster positive relationships, promote nurturing environments that increase belonging and inclusion, and provide us with rich learning experiences and knowledge development to assist us in better tackling life's challenges together.

Creating Space to Solve Problems: The AREA Method Backstory

I came to my interest in decision-making styles through thinking, writing, and teaching about solving complex problems, which ultimately led me to develop my own decision-making methodology, which I call the AREA Method. AREA was driven by my desire for greater confidence and conviction in my own decision-making. I wanted a systematic way to collect and analyze data, include stakeholder perspectives, and make at least some of my mistakes *before* making them, by checking and challenging my biases, assumptions, and judgments. As I began working with others to help them with their big decisions, I realized that people needed a way to sit with the material on their own, so I ultimately authored two books about AREA. The first, *Problem Solved: A Powerful System for Making Complex Decisions with Confidence and Conviction,* focused on personal and professional decision-making; the second, *Investing in Financial Research: A Decision-Making System for Better Results,* focused on conducting business, economic, and investment research to make financial decisions.

It all began when I was fresh out of graduate school and spent a decade as an investigative journalist, editor, and columnist for the business magazine *Barron's*. The idea for AREA initially came to me because I ended up specializing in what was called the "bearish" company story. Bearish stories take a skeptical look at a company's financials or strategy. When my stories were published, there was often a large share-price reaction. At times, an exchange halted trading in the stock, or regulators got involved. In a few cases, the companies I investigated and wrote about went out of business. In one case, the chief executive was sentenced to ten years in jail.

I became concerned about the human toll of my stories, so I wanted to ensure that I was conducting sound research. I wanted to take into account the incentives and motives of my sources, think about the quality of the evidence I gathered to back my assertions, and ensure that I was considering where I might be biased and judgmental in how I looked at and interpreted the data. That's how I came to the idea of the perspective-taking that frames my AREA Method.

The AREA Method gets its name from the different decision steps and perspectives it addresses. AREA is an acronym for these perspectives: Absolute, Relative, Exploration and Exploitation, and Analysis.

The first "A," or "Absolute," refers to primary, uninfluenced information from the source or sources at the center of your research. "R," or "Relative," refers to the perspectives of outsiders around your research subject. It is secondary information, or information that has been filtered through sources connected to your subject. "E," or "Exploration and Exploitation," represents the twin engines of creativity, one being about expanding your research breadth and the other about depth. Exploration moves your research beyond document-based sources to teach you to listen to other peoples' perspectives by developing sources and interviewing. Exploitation asks you to focus inward, on you as the decision maker, to examine how you process information, exploring and challenging your own assumptions and judgment. The second "A," "Analysis," is the final step in the process, when you synthesize the information you've collected to make your decision.

Until AREA, there was no system to control for and counter cognitive biases and mental mistakes in decision-making. Expert psychologists such as Daniel Kahnaman (*Thinking Fast and Slow*) and Robert Cialdini (*Influence*) showed us that we are all likely to commit thinking mistakes, but they left us with the problem and no solution. At its crux, AREA uses perspective-taking and an order of operations that teaches us to both separate our sources of information so that we sit in each point of view and also get distance on our own thinking and data processing. It's the opposite of Google, where we plug in a few search terms and are immediately flooded with results and no way to interpret the data. The distinction is stark. Instead of a cacophony of voices, AREA leads to decisions that are inclusive and built on a collaborative backbone. It solves problems holistically and provides guardrails against faulty thinking.

As I brought AREA out in the world, the system attracted far wider adoption than I had anticipated. It's been implemented by students in meditation study groups, world-class universities, and underresourced high schools; employees in and leaders of nonprofit agencies; government organizations; start-ups, small- and medium-sized businesses, and global multinational companies; and members of the military and intelligence communities.

From working with so many different types of people, I've seen AREA applied to a diverse range of decisions from deeply personal ones such as whether a teen felt comfortable living with his mother, to broad national security decisions about how to improve counterterrorism strategies in the Middle East and North Africa. Families have used AREA to think about college choices; an MIT professor used it to plan how to become—as he puts it—a more "interesting" person; an award-winning documentary filmmaker employed AREA to help him conduct research for his latest documentary film; and the chief executive and founder of a start-up company applied AREA to develop a go-to-market strategy for a complicated artificial intelligence technology.

As I worked with such diverse users, I realized that some parts of the system were easier for some people than others, which led me to think about the different ways that people approach decision-making and what kinds of data they were most attracted to.

In other words, *how* AREA worked often seemed to vary from person to person. The finance and investment experts loved the approach to investigating numbers but weren't sold on some of the interpersonal steps. The intelligence community glommed onto the creative exercises but sped through the Absolute part of the process because they thought they knew all of that information already. The high school and university communities, while so different from each other, wanted to jump to literature reviews—the type of research they were accustomed to—before really nailing down their vision of success.

AREA is set up to overcome biases in thinking and decision-making, but I began to see that decision makers would benefit from something immediate—something more personal about their decision-making approach—before they began their problem-solving so that they could truly implement AREA effectively. Beginning with yourself—doing the research on your own thinking and feelings about your decisions first—helps you make decisions more mindfully and more effectively.

We are not all subject to the same cognitive biases. Identifying and understanding which ones tend to trip us up, when, and why can help us use AREA as a compass to safely navigate through those individual crosswinds.

How do we better understand our own process of reasoning and making decisions so that we may tailor our application of decision-making skills and strategies to make better decisions for who we are specifically? That's been a missing piece in decision science.

Using the original research from all of the groups I worked with, I studied these findings using my background in investigative journalism and my years of research experience around decision-making, which had given me a skill set for collecting, organizing, analyzing, and communicating information. I also teamed up with researchers from MIT's Poverty Action Lab and Berkeley's Greater Good Science Center to develop an evaluation system to measure the growth in users' decision-making skills before and after using AREA.

The evaluation that we constructed captured data around the core underpinnings of AREA's basic principles, including controlling for and countering cognitive bias, spotting assumption and judgment, viewing stakeholder perspectives, focusing on incentives and motives, conducting research, and incorporating strategic stops into decision-making to analyze findings. In addition to anonymized written surveys, I also interviewed selected AREA users to better understand their responses and experience immediately after using the system, at six months, and again a year later. Looking at all of this data, I began to recognize five distinct decision-making archetypes.

As I was pulling all of this research together, I began to see that I needed to give users the tools to derive their own decision-making style themselves. Much as I had created AREA so that everyone would have the tools to make complex personal and professional decisions on their own, I wanted to develop a tool that would allow anyone to learn more about themselves as a decision maker and to learn about the different ways that people approach problem solving. I knew that if I developed a tool that needed my involvement it would limit the tool's reach and perhaps even bias the outcome of any research.

The Origins of the Problem Solver Profile

At this point in time Andrew Mangino, the chief executive and cofounder of the Future Project, a national nonprofit that works in high schools to promote a growth mindset in young adults, approached me. He said he'd read *Problem Solved* and that "the number one request that I get from high school principals is for help with decision-making for their students."

Could AREA be adapted for high school students? I was game. I began thinking about how teens and young adults like to spend their time and turned not to the college and graduate students in my classes but instead to the three students I knew best: my own kids. My son was busy with his favorite pastime: PlayStation. I found my answer: I'd gamify the interview process and create software that could be used anywhere.

I was excited to develop a high school version of AREA, but my research into decision-making archetypes led me to recognize that this was the perfect opportunity to also introduce this new concept. Adolescents, in the early stages of identity formation, are ripe to want to know more about themselves. Sharing insights into the way they tend to approach problem solving with its associated decision strengths and blind spots seemed perfect for teens navigating their way to adulthood. In addition, adolescents are used to being exposed to new tools and techniques that help them understand their learning styles to promote effective learning.

The PSP made its debut on a rainy Sunday in March 2017 when I held a half-day "boot camp" for teens gathered from two high schools: a charter school in Newark and a community arts school in Brooklyn. The students were immediately engaged. Over the course of the day, they tackled questions such as "How do I make friends at the new school I'm going to next year?" and "Can I continue to live with my mom?" They quickly understood, as one student put it, "I need to think before I do," and that, as another said, "Not making a decision is actually a BIG decision." By the end of the day, one student had come to this important realization: "I'm too dependent on my parents and I need to stop that." Another student observed, "There are good and bad choices, and how we get to the answers is imperative to growing." Perhaps my favorite observation of the day was this: "Since the only thing we really have control over is our choices, it made me even more excited about what my future will hold."

In a survey conducted at the end of the workshop, all of the students said it had been a valuable experience and 100 percent reported that they would recommend it to a friend.

A few days later, I spoke with one of the teachers who'd been in attendance. She told me, "Students have been referencing their decision-maker style from the app with other students at school—and getting really excited about it. They say that knowing their decision-maker type increases their awareness about the kinds of cognitive biases that might impact them the most so that they can control for and counteract some mental mistakes."

Since that first experience, I've incorporated the Problem Solver Profile module into almost all of my AREA work. It's as useful for CEOs and counterterrorism professionals as it is for high school students. The module begins with a quiz where users need to respond to eighteen statements with a yes or no answer. I encourage you to take the quiz when you finish reading this chapter. If you have questions as to why certain statements are included, go to the appendix or visit area-method.com.

A few pro tips: Answer the questions for what you do, not what you wish you did. The quiz is not proscriptive—and you are not limited by whatever you learn about yourself. Actually, in contrast, your new awareness can help you not only consider how you make decisions but how those with whom you make decisions approach their problem solving. Even better, you'll have some knowledge about what other decision-making styles look like, how to adopt them yourself, and the situations when you might want to use each. You'll also gain insight into the strengths and potential pitfalls of each approach.

PSPs are akin to handedness: most of us have a strong preference for using our right or left hand, and everything feels easier with that dominant hand. PSPs are ways of being that feel natural. They are behavioral responses, often instinctive, that you can lean on without needing to think about them.

But like the righty baseball player who learns to bat left, you too have capabilities you haven't developed. And like a baseball player who develops this versatile combination of skills, it will take time and practice—and discomfort—to become a decision-making switch-hitter.

The first step is to discover your dominant Problem Solver Profile.

PSP Quiz Instructions

1. Using your phone, open the camera app and scan the QR code, or go directly to app.areamethod.com to take the quiz.
2. Tap the notification that pops up to open the app.areamethod.com link.
3. Once at app.areamethod.com, click "Find my PSP" and then "Sign Up." Follow the instructions to create a login.
4. Take the PSP quiz and answer YES or NO to each question.
5. Don't skip any questions; choose the best answer to each statement.
6. Remember: almost no one is just one kind of decision maker; we're all situational decision-makers. The quiz scoring will identify your most dominant approach to problem solving but will also show how you scored relative to the other four PSP archetypes so you may see how the other styles influence your decisions.
7. Once you have this information, let's look at how your Problem Solver Profile interacts with lexicon, situationality and community.

Chapter Two

Lexicon, Situationality, and Community

The unexamined life is not worth living.
—Socrates

Congratulations, You're a . . . . . . ?

Adventurer

Detective

Listener

Thinker

Visionary

When Ari discovered that he was a Visionary, his first thought was that it made sense. "I had not thought about what kind of a decision maker I was," he said, "but identifying myself as a Visionary felt very accurate." He had in the past tried to think about himself and analyze and assess his behavioral habits. "I took the Myers-Briggs test long ago and learned that I was an ENTJ (essentially a dominant take-charge personality), but it didn't help me in any practical way." He recognized himself in the Myers-Briggs assessment, a self-report questionnaire indicating differing psychological preferences in how people perceive the world and make decisions, and in it telling him that he was an extrovert and that he relied on intuition. But the test also told him that he was "logical," someone who liked structure and made decisions in a "thinking way." He didn't know how to integrate this seemingly contradictory information and, more importantly, how to translate it into behavior.

When he completed the Problem Solver Profile and read that he was a Visionary, the profile information felt immediately more actionable and useful to Ari. "Reading through the profile, I could see that I was more idealistic than I thought and less focused on people. The idea that I was strong on symbols really resonated."

"Like other Visionaries, I'm great at initiating projects but not so great at finishing them. I immediately began thinking about my management style and both how I use my time and what I prioritize. I saw that I often would leave it up to team members to carry out—and finish—plans that I started. I realized right away that I needed to start separating what is urgent from what is important. That clarity would affect how I managed meetings on a daily basis and what I would choose to focus my time on."

Like Ari, you may have taken Myers-Briggs or any handful of other assessments that provide you with a look at your psychological profile related to career interests, intelligence, problem-solving aptitude, mental health, relationship styles, commitment readiness, and even what kind of dog fits your lifestyle. All of them can provide you with important self-knowledge.

But having self-knowledge and using that knowledge to solve problems are two different things. We may have been taught that knowledge is power, but by itself knowledge is useless. Too often, we learn that we are "good with numbers" or "comfortable in crowds," but that tells us nothing about what to do when our "good with numbers" job also requires us to be "good with people." Or we learn that we are "comfortable in crowds," but knowing that doesn't help us when we're one on one with the car salesman. That kind of knowledge doesn't help us plan for our (unpredictable) future; it doesn't guide us how to think or behave differently so that the decisions we make are both thought out and satisfying.

The Problem Solver Profile is practical and actionable. It provides you with:

- A basic overview of your go-to decision-making strategies and habits
- The behavioral and decision-making strengths for your profile
- The thinking mistakes and shortcuts associated with each problem-solving style; the cognitive biases that can inhibit good decision-making

- Examples of Problem Solvers like you in action
- Models of famous decision makers who may share your profile

Of course you'll want to read your profile first. Go ahead! But don't stop there. Read through all of the profiles. There are three distinct and different benefits to understanding and being familiar with all five decision-making archetypes: discerning situationality, creating a shared lexicon, and building effective community.

Discerning Situationality

Decision-making is situational. Situationality refers to the time, place, and people around you when you are making a decision. You as a decision maker change over time, and you make decisions differently based on where you are (at work versus at home) and who you're deciding with.

So while there is a likely winner that is your dominant Problem Solver Profile, you may have one or even two other PSPs that are close contenders, depending on the situation.

For example, a professional money manager might have an easy time being an Adventurer in personal investing but may be a Listener when it comes to child-rearing decisions. The opposite may be true for a child psychologist. And often the PSP is not something that is rooted in expertise; your profile may have been formed through personal experience or family precedent. In other words, one money manager might be an Adventurer while her colleague is a Detective. Another example: there are plenty of people who have enough money to buy luxuries but instead operate from a mindset of scarcity because that was the model and mindset they grew up with. So reading about and understanding all of the decision-making approaches and tendencies can arm you to be a better decision maker in all situations. More on this important topic later in chapter 14: Situationality and Dynamic Decision-Making.

Creating a Shared Lexicon

"Lexicon" refers to the vocabulary that you use to communicate your thoughts and feelings. Vocabulary need not be oral; it encompasses actions as well as words.

As Nietzsche once observed, language can both reveal and conceal truth. We understand the world and our experiences in it through language. What I consider "rudeness" might be very different from what you consider "rudeness." And what I label as "polite behavior" you might label as "pretension." So the first step in managing a problem is naming it. Once we can put a label on something, we can better explore it and evaluate it.

Gary Chapman, in his book *The Five Languages of Love*, has given us a lexicon to talk about love languages and to understand that expressions of love take many different forms. Understanding our own love language is the first step toward understanding why we do the things we do to give and receive love, and then being able to express that to someone else.

Here are two examples of how we are disconnected when we don't have the language to understand and identify our behavior. My friend Ruth knew her husband loved her, but she didn't always feel his love. When she discovered that her love language was actually language—compliments and words of appreciation—she tried to get her husband to be more expressive. He struggled with this because it felt unnatural to him, and it wasn't his lexicon. So one night at the dinner table, when the whole family began to eat the meal Ruth had cooked, she said aloud, "Ruth, this chicken is delicious! Thank you so much for cooking such a tasty dinner." Her husband and children looked at her oddly, and she explained that the compliments made her feel appreciated. Despite her husband's discomfort with compliments, Ruth had come to understand that compliments were important to her, so she modeled the behavior that would make her feel loved, and slowly, her family began to incorporate words of appreciation into their dinnertime.

Another friend of mine used to put her purse down wherever she'd like when she came home from being out. At bedtime, she would discover the purse on her nightstand. It had been carefully placed there by her husband, Sam. For years, this irritated her and made her feel infantilized. But when she and her husband began learning about love languages, she saw that Sam expressed love through acts of service, and that moving her purse so that it was somewhere she would be sure to find it was his way of taking care of the wife he loved so much.

In both examples, putting a label on their love languages allowed my friends to better communicate and connect with the important people in their lives. We can't give and take love effectively—reciprocally—with another person unless we understand their lexicon—and they understand ours.

The same is true for knowing and working effectively with the other decision makers in your life. In the same way that my friend came to understand Sam's loving purse-relocation—his behavioral lexicon—you can begin to see that others in your life may not make decisions the same way you do, allowing you to better connect with others both personally and professionally. Knowing the other Problem Solver Profiles will enable you to see others' actions in the context of their style, not as a personal affront, antagonistic choice, or shortcoming.

Knowing your Problem Solver Profile can also help you understand why certain decision-making strategies feel "natural" while others feel uncomfortable and make you anxious. But understanding those weaknesses or anxieties enables you to face them directly and strengthen your decision-making. Think about it like physical exercise: weight lifters don't just lift heavier and heavier weights; they also work on uncomfortable mobility exercises because improving mobility makes them better weight lifters.

In Walter Isaacson's biography of Steve Jobs, the author recounts the tragic story of Jobs's fixed worldview when it came to his pancreatic cancer. Allegedly, Jobs delayed surgery to remove his tumor—the recommended treatment—for nine months. During that interim period, he attempted to treat his cancer with alternative medicine, including a special diet, according to news reports. Jobs was so sure of himself as a Visionary thinker who had changed the world technologically that he devalued other problem-solving approaches. With his cancer diagnosis, Jobs couldn't see that he might benefit from a different decision-making strategy for his health and medical care. He didn't need just a creative, out-of-the-box solution; he might have been helped more by a proven, evidence-based solution. If Jobs could have seen that what worked for him as a Visionary tech innovator was a weakness in approaching his own health, he might have made different decisions about his own health.

Community

Community is often defined as a social unit in which there is some commonality, such as norms, religion, values, customs, geography, or identity.

We recognize ourselves as being part of a religious community or a neighborhood or a school system, but we often miss the sense of community that is at the core of this book, namely, of problem-solving approaches.

The world is a diverse place, and while societies grapple with how to traverse the variety of experiences and identities, there are a few common tendencies across the human experience. We begin by seeing difference, and hopefully acknowledge that someone is from a different background. We can hear when someone is speaking a different language, so then we can begin to explore our reaction and open ourselves to our biases and work to change ourselves. But we carry other biases that we haven't—or don't easily—recognize.

With differences in decision-making style or even reading speed, we make the same uninformed judgments about others but don't recognize that our judgment is coming from a place of bias. In other words, because someone doesn't think or make decisions the way we do, we often make (wrong) assumptions about why they act the way they do. We may see an Adventurer as careless or a Listener as sheeplike or the Detective as stuck in the weeds because each of these individuals makes decisions differently than we do. But all decision-making strategies have value and utility.

For difference that you can see—and for difference that you can't see—the work begins with recognizing and celebrating difference and truly understanding that your way is neither better nor worse. One recent example: I've been doing the *New York Times* crossword puzzle with one of my daughters and am amazed that the same clue will lead each of us to a different answer. Just days ago, a clue read "Prince, e.g." with an eight-letter space. My answer: male heir; hers: handsome. Both fit! The correct answer was "male heir" but truthfully, her answers are right as often as mine.

Interestingly, diversity that is apparent often masks a lack of diversity around problem-solving styles or decision-making strengths and weaknesses. In my work with a variety of organizations, using the Problem Solver Profile with groups large and small, the results often show that there is one (very) dominant PSP within an organization even when it is composed of people with diverse backgrounds and experiences.

For example, I've given a few talks for IVY, an international organization that bills itself as a "lifelong university" offering a wide range of courses to "supercharge your life and career" and "elevate your leadership, performance and wellness." IVY's goal is to bring diverse minds together to learn with and from one another. I've presented to IVY groups on both coasts, and, looking around any of the workshops I've led, the attendees looked like a diverse group; they've ranged in age, gender, and ethnic and professional backgrounds. However, when I administered the Problem Solver Profile assessment, and then asked the takers to group themselves based on their PSP, every time we ended up with a huge clump of Thinkers. No other PSP group came even close to the size of the Thinker group—at every IVY presentation. By almost three to one, attendees had the same Thinker orientation for their decision-making. As a Detective myself, it was often mighty lonely in those workshops; in one, there was only a single other Detective out of about forty attendees.

Why does intellectual diversity of community matter? It matters because different decision makers will identify and ask different questions and will approach problems from a range of perspectives. When we create a community that is diverse in terms of intellectual exploration and decision-making styles, we will make more carefully thought-out community decisions, and ones that are more inclusive.

Improving the diversity of our decision-making communities also benefits us individually. We gain valuable practice in checking and challenging our own assumptions and judgments. Being exposed to and learning from other PSPs in turn not only helps us more fully evaluate a personal decision before it is made but also can improve our own creativity and innovation.

By surrounding yourself with people who value different aspects of the decision-making process—whether it's someone who listens while you're off gathering data or someone who trusts their gut while you like to evaluate the options before moving forward—you can build critical thinking skills and add nuance to your understanding of problems and possibilities.

There is no "sweet spot" between the different Problem Solver Profiles. While some decisions—or even different stages of a decision—might look like they are better made by certain PSPs, a decision's success not only benefits from creative tension between different decision approaches but also depends in part on what you or your team are solving for and what you, uniquely, deem to be a successful outcome.

As former secretary of defense Donald Rumsfeld once said, "You go to war with the army you have, not the army you might want or wish to have at a later time." It's not possible to assemble a team to anticipate every decision-making opportunity and situation. However, bringing different

PSPs together to tackle a decision can better check and challenge bias, assumption, and judgment than working with a team who all share the same PSP. Homogeneity in PSPs may end up potentially amplifying bias, as was the case with Ari and his team.

Some months after Ari took the Problem Solver Profile, I began working with him and his cofounder Tim, who had been Ari's college roommate. I was excited to work with two passionate young men who were pursuing this big dream to better the world. They had grand ideas, but it quickly became apparent that Ari and Tim had launched their charity without developing a targeted and focused plan.

They hadn't done what seemed like fairly basic research; they were so taken with the importance of stopping human trafficking that they set up their nonprofit without even first exploring other nonprofits operating in Ahmedabad or even successful models of anti–sex-trafficking charities in other places. And where did the model that they chose to follow come from? It was based on a history book that Ari happened to read on his flight home from his fateful trip to India.

Ari was reading *Rogue Heroes*, the story of the origins of the SAS, Britain's Special Air Service, started by a Visionary man, David Sterling. Sterling became convinced during World War II that, due to the mechanized nature of war, a small team of highly trained soldiers with the advantage of surprise could attack enemy targets. Operating outside of the traditional rules of military engagement, this team snuck behind enemy lines, collected information, and conducted (mostly successful) covert operations. This not only upended the balance of the war but forever changed the nature of combat itself—as Visionary a tale as one might find. Their motto was "Who dares, wins."

As more and more Visionary pieces seemed to be guiding Ari and Tim's Protect Her Life organization, I wanted to better understand Tim's perspective to help our work together and asked him to take the Problem Solver Profile test. The result was not surprising: Tim is a Visionary too.

With two Visionaries at the helm of a charity, there was no one to anchor their high-flying dreams to the reality of running a complex organization trying to solve an age-old, intractable problem.

Tim confessed that he had tried to "put the brakes on" some of Ari's big plans, but it felt both unnatural and uncomfortable. Tim was truly a wolf trying to wear the sheep's clothing: he couldn't pretend to be a Detective or a Thinker. "I would try, but I would let Ari's enthusiasm sweep me up. I quickly realized that I wanted to be overruled; I wanted to be on team Visionary."

When Ari found out that Tim was a Visionary, he laughed. It made so much sense and explained the power of their friendship: they both want to change the world. To their credit, once they were confronted with their homogenous PSPs, they quickly recognized that they needed someone—perhaps several someones—to check and challenge their processes and plans.

They had initially been working on an end-to-end solution for human trafficking that began with mapping criminal networks perpetrating these terrible crimes and ended with both rehabilitating the girls and women they helped free during police raids and aiding prosecutors in putting arrested criminals in jail. It was too much; it was everything Visionary, but how could one start-up bootstrapped charity do it all? We'll explore how Ari and Tim refined this expansive mission and what it meant to mitigate their PSP blind spots in practice and practical application in our upcoming chapters.

You and your spouse (or best friend or business co-owner) may find that you share the same Problem Solver Profile too, or that you inhabit different ones. Either way, you'll get to know one another at a different and deeper level. As educator Horace Mann once said, "Every addition to true knowledge is an addition to power."

Welcome to the world of diverse decision-making profiles.

Chapter Three

The Adventurer

Courage is the price that life exacts for granting peace.
—Amelia Earhart

You make decisions quickly and you trust your gut feeling. When faced with a challenge, big or small, you'd rather do what feels right than spend your time thinking through all the choices. You know who you are, and you know what you want—so you aren't afraid to go get it.

Strengths

Being the Adventurer comes with a lot of perks. One of your defining strengths is your confidence—you believe in yourself, and you know what you stand for. That's a powerful thing! This confidence probably shows up in your life in a lot of ways, including when you've got a big decision ahead of you. You are not afraid to make big decisions, and you don't concern yourself with how others might make the same decision. Another defining strength is that you are built for speed—you move quickly! You aren't afraid to go boldly toward what you want, and fast. That lets you get a lot done in a short period of time, and can mean you're fun to be around—always up for something new, and often high-energy.

Blind Spots

There are some downfalls to this Problem Solver Profile too. Your confidence can make you believe that things are going to go your way—and sometimes they won't, especially when you don't have data to back your decision. This **optimism bias** makes you feel unstoppable, which sometimes can lead you into danger. Because you like to move quickly, and are optimistic about pretty much everything, you don't always have an accurate sense of how long something really takes. This **planning fallacy** means you run the risk of falling behind schedule and not actually accomplishing everything you want to. Because you have such strong beliefs in what is right and what is wrong, you aren't always able to look at the full picture. Sometimes, you'll see evidence that tells you that you're going in the wrong direction, but your **confirmation bias** leads you to find a way to make it support what you think is right. And when a decision truly should involve others, you often don't want to take the time to listen, tuning out those close to you because you think you already know what they're going to say. This **closeness-communication bias** can harm relationships and prevent others from buying in to your decisions. Watch out for these biases that you have—if you know what they are, you can make sure to protect yourself from them!

Adventurers in Action

Baba's Example

Fifty-year-old Baba doesn't look at first blush like an Adventurer. He'd been a senior accountant at one of the largest accounting firms in the country. He'd worked for the same firm for most of his career. However, as a first-generation American, born to South Asian immigrant parents, Baba had to tamp down his Adventurer tendencies in order to meet his parents' expectations. He worked for decades at a job he didn't enjoy. But when COVID hit, and he was laid off and faced with the big decision of what to do next with his life, his Adventurer self took over.

Baba thought he was interested in economics and wanted the cachet of a top program, so he googled "Masters in Applied Economics" and was excited to see that Johns Hopkins offered one. He applied—to only that program—was accepted, and started, without even looking to see what jobs the program's graduates obtained or even who recruited on campus. All he needed, he thought, was the first step (the Hopkins degree) and everything else would fall into place.

Baba found himself in school without ever stopping to think about what he actually wanted to do after graduation. That's when he found me. He read an article that I'd written, saw that I did career counseling, and decided to get in touch.

As we began to work together, Baba recognized that his optimism bias combined with his desire to move quickly through the decision-making process and his belief in his "trust your gut" style had combined to prevent him from taking the careful steps to think about what he truly wanted to accomplish in his life. He was excited to be released from a job he hated, and any kind of careful thinking about the future felt too much like being chained down again.

Although he recognized that he'd rushed to a decision about Hopkins, when I tried to pin him down about how he'd know that the decision had been a success, week in and week out, he couldn't articulate a response. He didn't know what he wanted from the degree. Instead, he came to me each week with new ideas (unrelated to the degree he was pursuing) for what to do with his future—everything from opening a swimming school in his home country to joining a day-trading firm to opening a gourmet food truck that would serve South Asian dishes.

It all sounded great—and certainly I could see that his plans included many elements of a good life: fitness, financial acumen, and fine food. However, his vision also clearly suffered from healthy doses of planning fallacy in addition to the optimism bias. When I asked him how he would choose which path he would pursue and whether there should be an order of priorities, he gave a very adventurous answer: "I don't want to choose."

Adventurers often feel that they shouldn't have to choose, that life has a lot to offer, and they want to grab as much as they can. Moving slowly, in an Adventurer's mind, is for tortoises and slugs. They optimistically believe they can move forward on gut reaction and will see what "sticks."

What Baba needed was to feel like he was moving forward. Ultimately Adventurers fear getting stuck in the details for too long. However, there are times where even an Adventurer's confidence has to be enriched with some data, so we worked together to channel his enthusiasm into a few research questions that got to the core of his decision problem and gave him a sense of momentum toward his goals.

I guided Baba to consider whether it might be feasible to pursue more than one dream at a time. I suggested he conduct research into whether it would be practical to work two jobs. He liked this idea a lot.

Baba investigated whether, after graduation, he could join a financial company that had a stock-trading training program during weekday traditional working hours and then possibly operate a food truck on select evenings or weekends. By committing to researching both decisions at once, we checked and challenged his tendency as an Adventurer to move both quickly and in diverse directions. Was there evidence that could shed light on his optimism bias for how and why his ambitious idea might (or might not) succeed?

The truth is that probably a lot of day traders and food truck owners *are* Adventurers. Both are entrepreneurial activities with a high risk of failure, likely to draw optimistic, risk-taking individuals like Baba. An entrepreneur who opens a restaurant franchise like a Subway, rather than an independent restaurant, takes a lot less risk. A franchise has the brand-name recognition and the large supervising organization behind it, with all the scaffolding that entails—tested training programs as well as policies and practices previously proven successful.

Ultimately, and in true Adventurer form, Baba found the spadework necessary to think through his options too overwhelming and he gave up. He decided instead to just focus on his schoolwork and the part-time job he had taken to help pay the bills. But within just days of that update, he reached out to share that he had a new adventure in mind: "I'm working on an idea now with a couple of my professors. I will reach out to you when it's time to build the business plan."

When working with an Adventurer, remember to be positive and have empathy for the Adventurer's bold spirit. Identifying and channeling their motivation will make them feel understood and will give you a seat on an exciting plane ride.

Doris's Example

Doris, an Adventurer, loves her daughter, Sharon, a Detective, very much and became extremely protective of her daughter during Sharon's difficult and contentious divorce trial. When Sharon's eldest child graduated from high school, it was going to be the first time the divided family all gathered together. Sharon wanted to keep the spotlight on her son, Danny, and knew Doris's Adventurer tendencies, so she spoke with her mom several times about the importance of not engaging with Sharon's ex at the graduation. Doris assured Sharon in these conversations that she understood the plan and signed on. But on the fateful day, just as everyone took their seats and the graduates were lined up to process in, Doris marched over to Sharon's ex, his new girlfriend, his parents, and his brother's family and cursed him out loudly.

Doris's closeness-communication bias led her to believe that even though Sharon had expressly asked her *not* to make a fuss, Doris should tune out that request. She was so certain that making a fuss was the right thing to do. Sharon's ex could not get a free pass. When else would Doris have a chance to express her anger and disgust with him?

Sharon was horrified and embarrassed; her other children felt torn between their parents. They wanted all to be well for their graduating brother.

This is another downside of the Adventurer: Adventurers can be so certain of themselves and the rightness of their ideas and actions that they can be thoughtless and hurtful.

Doris's determination to avenge her daughter's pain instead resulted in more pain, sadness, and humiliation for Sharon and for Doris's grandchildren. If you have an Adventurer parent or spouse, you may well recognize

---

A FEW TIPS FOR ADVENTURERS

- Pay attention to your first inclination. What is your gut suggesting you do? Then consider how that's worked out in the past for *this particular type of decision.* Your Adventurer spirit might be great for some decisions but not for others. If this type of decision is one that hasn't gone well for you in the past, check your instincts with data or with someone who knows you well as a decision maker.
- Pay attention to the other stakeholders involved in your decision. Are you running roughshod over them? Make time to listen to them without judgment. To truly solve a problem that involves others, we need to include those people involved.
- Since Adventurers like to keep moving forward, try to remember that the present is "the present." Don't stint on your now just to get to an imagined future.

this type of situation. If you are an Adventurer, when it comes to speaking your mind, you don't always know what is best for other people. It is one thing to make decisions for yourself, but be careful when taking unilateral action on behalf of others.

Three Famous People Who Could Be Adventurers

Amelia Earhart, aviation pioneer; Roxane Gay, writer, professor, and editor; and Ernest Shackleton, Antarctic explorer

What Makes Ernest Shackleton an Adventurer?

Sir Ernest Henry Shackleton is best known as a polar explorer. He was associated with four expeditions exploring Antarctica, particularly the Trans-Antarctic (Endurance) Expedition (1914–16) that he led, which, although unsuccessful, became famous as a tale of remarkable perseverance and survival. He is remembered as someone who was good at improvisation and an instinctual leader. According to biographer Michael Smith, Shackleton was "a man not afraid to throw away the rulebook or abandon plans if they were not working. He was a man for a tight spot."

Sir Raymond Priestley, the acclaimed scientist who served on multiple Antarctic expeditions with a variety of leaders including Robert Scott, Roald Amundsen, and Shackleton, once wrote: "For scientific leadership, give me Scott. For swift and efficient travel, Amundsen. But when you are in a hopeless situation, when there seems no way out, get on your knees and pray for Shackleton." Alas, it all didn't end well for Shackleton; while he explored areas that other people were afraid to go to, this adventurous streak also led him to be restless and make decisions so quickly that his business ventures failed. Learn from his boldness and from his mistakes.

Why Is Amelia Earhart an Adventurer?

It takes a deep belief in your own skills and talents to decide that you will be the first woman to fly solo across the Atlantic Ocean. Adventurers are willing to take a leap of faith even when they don't have evidence to support their decisions—and that optimism bias is what can bolster their success or undermine their dreams.

Earhart certainly didn't have evidence to support her dream of flying, which was a brand-new field during her lifetime, but she wasn't afraid to break down barriers. As a teen, she kept a scrapbook filled with news clippings of independent, successful women. She followed in their footsteps, becoming, in 1923, only the sixteenth woman in the world to receive a pilot's license.

She also made a noticeable impact on key aviation safety regulations, which were not yet in place when she was flying. During one especially turbulent flight, her map blew off her lap in her open airplane. She soon realized that there were no visible landmarks to direct her toward a safe airfield. She later advocated for painting town names on signs in bright colors to assist lost pilots in flight.

Earhart's ambitious nature allowed her to achieve remarkable feats, from her first solo flight to her attempted circumnavigation of the world, which sadly led to her mysterious disappearance. Yet it was her willingness to be bold and venture into the unknown, despite the constant threat of physical danger and judgment from those who discouraged women with nontraditional aspirations, which ensured her far-reaching legacy.

Is Roxane Gay an Adventurer?

Some Adventurers scale mountains, while others use their strong opinions to share innovative ideas. Gay's writing represents the intersection of bold ideas and a confidence to move forward swiftly that is common with Adventurers. She is the author of many books, including her *New York Times* best-selling essay collection *Bad Feminist*. *Slate* magazine's review says that the essays "rarely deposit you at a destination. Gay's essays are more beginnings and middles than they are ends," a perfect description of how the Adventurer has lots of ideas and likes to keep moving forward to what is next.

A profile written about her in the *Guardian* said Gay is "someone who has seen a lot and takes no prisoners." Adventurers can be both refreshing and aggressive or uncompromising in the pursuit of their objectives.

Chapter Four

The Detective

I am turned into a sort of machine for observing facts and grinding out conclusions.
–Charles Darwin

You value information and are always looking for the facts and the data. You don't make your decisions based on how you feel—you want to see what the evidence says, and you listen to it. You believe that the more you learn and soak in the details, the better you'll do—and you're committed to gathering as much information as you can.

Strengths

Being the Detective means that you are committed to getting the facts, which means that you tend to have more factual information and data than the people around you. But you don't like just *any* facts; you tend to prefer expert data rather than opinions from friends. You are focused when you are faced with a decision. You don't let your emotions distract you, or deny that they can, and that means you can thoughtfully look at the evidence you uncover. You don't expect to know everything because you know that you can find the information that you need when you need it—through research. You are down to earth, and you don't settle for nonsense. You don't have a problem making a decision once you feel like you have the right information.

Blind Spots

Being a Detective comes with a few drawbacks too. Sometimes, you focus so heavily on gathering evidence that you don't know when to stop, and the amount of information leads you to lose sight of the forest (decision context) because you're so focused on the trees (data). This **frame blindness** can mean that you miss the bigger picture, leading to complications such as solving the wrong problem or only part of the problem that you are grappling with. More information does not always make for a better decision. Detectives can also fall prey to **confirmation bias**, cherry-picking through reams of data to support a favored hypothesis. More information is not always unbiased information. Published research is often not the only type of information out there. You can learn from your Listener friends and colleagues the value of others' opinions and experiences. Further, Detectives, so comfortable with data, often lead with it and think others value it as well, falling prey to **projection bias**, thinking that others prioritize it in the same way. By starting with data when making decisions with others, Detectives can come across as though they are not seeing the situation holistically and certainly not connecting to the people they are working with. For example, Detectives sometimes try to use data to solve problems that are probably better solved with "gut feelings." This is missing the emotional forest for the factual trees. Finally, because you like to soak up lots of information, you sometimes don't do a good job with time management; this **planning fallacy** means that you get so focused on learning that you don't make your decision on time.

Detectives in Action

Cheryl's Example

Because Detectives are so comfortable with documents and research, they often notice discrepancies and red flags that an Adventurer or Thinker might not see.

For example, I was reading a document written by the World Bank, which is tasked with fighting poverty in developing nations. I was curious about their investment policy and performance, and wondered how they decided whether an investment was truly making a difference. As a Detective, I of course read the footnotes in the article. One of those footnotes read:

> DOTS *ratings are company- rather than project-based and use proxies (e.g. annual returns on invested capital) rather than the more in-depth evaluation methods (e.g. life-of-project re-estimated financial and economic returns) used at the evaluation stage.*

In other words, the World Bank was making investments without measuring the success—or failure—of those investments. Instead, it tracked and measured the performance of the *whole company* that received the money, such as the Coca-Cola Company or Newmont Mining.

The article I wrote for *Foreign Policy* magazine, called "Can You Fight Poverty with a Five-Star Hotel?" questioned whether the World Bank was fulfilling its lofty mission. It was an important financial story that hadn't been told. However, Detectives' comfort with research and data can misfire in some situations.

Aanya's Example

Aanya, a physician who made her name in medical research, had worked her way up to running her department at a small academic hospital. When a patient at the hospital died unexpectedly and the family went public with it, Aanya was tasked with drafting the hospital's public response to explain what had happened and restore trust in the institution. The letter she drafted and subsequently sent out began with a barrage of numerical data establishing the department's commitment to patient care and their overall success. Needless to say, the patient's family felt neither comforted nor connected with this letter, and the larger community also responded negatively. Where was the humanity in what should have been an acknowledgment of grief and suffering?

Aanya the Detective was so reassured by the data that her frame blindness prevented her from recognizing that data wasn't an effective way to connect to other human beings—and in fact had the opposite effect. While doctors deal in facts, they are in the end dealing with people, who, by the nature of needing a hospital, are vulnerable.

TIPS FOR GETTING DETECTIVES OUT OF THE DATA WEEDS

- Ask why: Consider why the problem exists and what data will help you arrive at a solution. This may help the Detective see beyond data to better plumb the problem's root cause. As you collect data, ask yourself, does this data have diagnosticity? Check your data's ability to solve your problem.
- Search for multiple dimensions of a problem. Don't oversimplify. Problems can have many dimensions and many other stakeholders. Your decisions are not yours alone, even when they feel very personal. Data alone, in most cases, isn't enough to solve a complex problem.
- Tune in to your emotions and the emotions of other stakeholders involved in a decision. The emotional component of decision-making can be a real blind spot.

Three Famous People Who Could Be Detectives

Marie Curie, Nobel Prize–winning scientist; Charles Darwin, naturalist, geologist, biologist, evolutionary; and Ida B. Wells, suffragist and civil rights leader

Why Is Marie Curie a Detective?

Marie Curie was the only woman to ever win two Nobel Prizes. She did it by systematically gathering data and testing it out. She kept all her notes in journals that are now regarded as scientific and national treasures, but kept in lead-lined boxes at France's Bibliothèque nationale in Paris because they are still, after a hundred years, contaminated by radiation (the half-life of radium 226 is 1,600 years). The result of Curie's research was the discovery of not one but two new elements: polonium and radium.

What Makes Charles Darwin a Detective?

Darwin was certainly an observer, studying the natural world carefully and closely. His work on evolution and natural selection are foundational scientific concepts that are still used today. However, Darwin didn't observe the world around him for pleasure. His careful observations focused on gathering as much data as possible until he could draw a conclusion—the more he knew, the better!

For example, Darwin devoted eight years of his life to studying barnacle crustaceans. He spent every day dissecting, classifying, and writing about different species of barnacles. The four books he published on this subject made him a renowned figure in the British zoological community. Studying a group of organisms in such depth, both in their living and fossilized forms, allowed Darwin to observe and understand how the diversity of a species had developed over time. Darwin's Detective patience, attention to detail, and critical thinking helped him see something no one else had seen: evolution of species.

Why Is Ida B. Wells a Detective?

Balancing her time as a teacher and a journalist, Ida B. Wells was always searching for more information. When facing difficult stories of Black families in the South, Wells was able to navigate her emotions to stick to the facts she collected in her interviews, even though her work began after several friends were lynched in Tennessee. Her published reports of lynching brought an international awareness to the inhumane practice. She said the purpose of her book, *Lynch Law in Georgia*, was "to give the public the facts, in the belief that there is still a sense of justice in the American people, and that it will yet assert itself in condemnation of outlawry and in defense of oppressed and persecuted humanity." Her writing reflected her strengths as a Detective, always focused on the facts in front of her, taking her time to make sure that she had gathered the details and recorded them accurately.

positions of power, an example of **authority bias,** but also because you are loyal to those you trust, you can have a blind spot and make decisions based on what—or who!—you like, rather than on what's actually best. This is called the **liking bias.** In addition, because you like to listen to others, hearing their stories may lead you to the **narrative bias,** where you overvalue story lines and undervalue data. When you pay too much attention to what others are thinking and doing, you can stop thinking for yourself. This **social proof bias** means that you may be swayed to do what others recommend, instead of thinking about what you actually want.

Listeners in Action

Flor's Example

Flor, a Listener who is a mid-level technology executive at a global financial institution, was tasked as a point person in charge of coordinating across departments with an outside vendor for a new software implementation. During her calls with the vendor's project manager, Randi, Flor was constantly faced with decisions that needed to be made. She freely shared her thoughts with Randi and then, after the call, reported back across the bank's internal team to relay what had transpired in the conversations. Once she received internal feedback, Flor would write a follow-up email to Randi, updating her with the action plan. T̶ often differed from what Randi and Flor had discussed i̶

Flor thought the project was going well until o̶n̶ whether she had the authority to make un̶i̶l̶a̶t̶
̶h̶e̶ d̶i̶d̶n̶ ̶s̶ as a po̶i̶

Chapter Five

The Listener

For every one of us that succeeds, it's because there's somebody there to show you the way out.
—Oprah Winfrey

You've got a whole village of people in your life whom you trust and who support you. When you are faced with a challenge or a decision, you know you can rely on your people. They love you, and you love them— and it means you always have a plethora of advice ready for you when you ask. You don't have to make a decision by yourself.

more powerful than having a tight network
who support you. As a Listener, your

Strengths

In life, there are few things [...]
of people whom you support and w[...]
community is one of your biggest assets. You have people w[...]
to help you make decisions and move forward in your life. Y[...]
you can always turn to them. That is a great position to be i[...]
you are a trusting person who believes in the people around y[...]
no trouble building relationships with people and continuin[...]
your network of support.

Blind Spots

Being a Listener means that you may rely too heavily on o[...]
to make decisions for you. Not only may you be swayed by[...]

. This plan
n their call.
e day Randi asked her
material decisions. Flor told her that
role was a point of contact, just as Randi's was. Randi then
e was both the project manager and manager for her team's
been acting on Flor's decisions, only to have to undo or change
eam was taking after Flor's follow-up emails arrived.
surprised. What had seemed to her Listener self like good
come across to Randi as final decisions. Taking this new
g into account, Flor apologized and suggested that Randi
etailed agenda items for the calls. She wanted to know what
eded to be made and the time line for those decisions. That
Flor to assess whether she would be able to make decisions
and when to invite other division leaders onto the call when

Chapter Five

The Listener

For every one of us that succeeds, it's because there's somebody
there to show you the way out.
–Oprah Winfrey

You've got a whole village of people in your life whom you trust and who support you. When you are faced with a challenge or a decision, you know you can rely on your people. They love you, and you love them— and it means you always have a plethora of advice ready for you when you ask. You don't have to make a decision by yourself.

Strengths

In life, there are few things more powerful than having a tight network of people whom you support and who support you. As a Listener, your community is one of your biggest assets. You have people whom you trust to help you make decisions and move forward in your life. You know that you can always turn to them. That is a great position to be in. In general, you are a trusting person who believes in the people around you. You have no trouble building relationships with people and continuing to expand your network of support.

Blind Spots

Being a Listener means that you may rely too heavily on other people to make decisions for you. Not only may you be swayed by people in positions of power, an example of **authority bias,** but also because you are loyal to those you trust, you can have a blind spot and make decisions based on what—or who!—you like, rather than on what's actually best. This is called the **liking bias.** In addition, because you like to listen to others, hearing their stories may lead you to the **narrative bias,** where you overvalue story lines and undervalue data. When you pay too much attention to what others are thinking and doing, you can stop thinking for yourself. This **social proof bias** means that you may be swayed to do what others recommend, instead of thinking about what you actually want.

Listeners in Action

Flor's Example

Flor, a Listener who is a mid-level technology executive at a global financial institution, was tasked as a point person in charge of coordinating across departments with an outside vendor for a new software implementation. During her calls with the vendor's project manager, Randi, Flor was constantly faced with decisions that needed to be made. She freely shared her thoughts with Randi and then, after the call, reported back across the bank's internal team to relay what had transpired in the conversations. Once she received internal feedback, Flor would write a follow-up email to Randi, updating her with the action plan. This plan often differed from what Randi and Flor had discussed in their call.

Flor thought the project was going well until one day Randi asked her whether she had the authority to make unilateral decisions. Flor told her that she didn't. Her role was as a point of contact, just as Randi's was. Randi then shared that she was both the project manager and manager for her team's work and had been acting on Flor's decisions, only to have to undo or change the path the team was taking after Flor's follow-up emails arrived.

Flor was surprised. What had seemed to her Listener self like good listening had come across to Randi as final decisions. Taking this new understanding into account, Flor apologized and suggested that Randi send more detailed agenda items for the calls. She wanted to know what decisions needed to be made and the time line for those decisions. That would allow Flor to assess whether she would be able to make decisions on her own and when to invite other division leaders onto the call when she couldn't. By having a detailed agenda ahead of time, Flor could also discuss division leaders' concerns prior to the call with Randi so that she could convey their wishes on the call. Flor also committed to letting Randi know before a call ended when she felt that she needed to go back to her group before signing off on a decision.

For Flor, the process was more laborious and the longer calls with more people felt more difficult, but she could see that Randi was practiced and comfortable in this group dynamic and worked well to achieve the consensus that was so important for Flor's company.

Part of the difficulty for Flor and Randi was that Flor gave the impression that the decision had been made when it had not. Flor was unaware that this was creating problems for Randi, her team, and the pace of the project. As a Listener, be aware of your language around decision-making. Are you giving the impression to someone that a decision has been made when you intend to canvass others?

Linda's Example

Linda was part of her neighborhood association because she loved her neighborhood. One day, when checking her email she noticed a chain of angry emails that had been initiated by an older gentleman, Irwin. He chastised neighborhood walkers who were walking, in his opinion, too far out into the street. There were no sidewalks, so the street had to accommodate both cars and walkers. Linda read through the angry responses and worried that this small controversy would spiral into long-standing bad feelings. As a Listener, Linda thought Irwin's initial email might have come from a place of worry and that his "anger" was concern that he might hit a pedestrian with his car. She volunteered to speak in person with Irwin so that the situation would not escalate. As a Listener, she was comfortable talking to someone, even someone who appeared angry and confrontational.

Three Famous People with Listener Traits

Mahatma Gandhi, pacifist leader of India; Nelson Mandela, anti-apartheid revolutionary and first president of South Africa; and Oprah Winfrey, media personality and businesswoman icon

Why Is Mahatma Gandhi a Listener?

Mahatma Gandhi was able to change India through nonviolence because of his ability to listen to others and understand the needs of his people and their arguments. In turn his listening enabled him to be persuasive and able to reason and negotiate between conflicting parties, whether it was Muslims and Hindus, or between the British government and its Indian subjects.

HOW LISTENERS CAN BETTER IDENTIFY THEIR OWN INNER VOICE

- Before listening to others, listen first to yourself. What is your end goal? For Listeners, using a notebook can be helpful: by writing down the problem as well as your goals, you'll have a concrete record to serve as a check against letting others' opinions sway you too far.
- Use your notebook as a record of your emotions as well. Can you identify and make explicit what you are feeling about a decision and about working with the stakeholders involved? Your emotions are both a leading indicator and a feedback mechanism. What might they be trying to tell you about the decision you face, and how do you want to engage with them?
- As you reach out to speak with others about your decision, be clear to lead with your goals so that other people respond to your incentives and motives instead of theirs.

Was Nelson Mandela a Listener?

Listeners are strong leaders because they are able to navigate the needs and desires of multiple perspectives. Nelson Mandela mastered this skill and changed the course of his native South Africa forever. As he once told Oprah, another great Listener, "I learned to have the patience to listen when people put forward their views, even if I think those views are wrong. You can't reach a just decision in a dispute unless you listen to both sides, ask questions, and view the evidence placed before you. If you don't allow people to contribute, to offer their point of view, or to criticize what has been put before them, then they can never like you. And you can never build that instrument of collective leadership."[1]

Mandela did just that. After being imprisoned for several decades, he navigated governing in the era after apartheid as the first Black head of state building trust with a diverse group of allies. He was able to bring together people who had previously been at odds because of his skills as a listener.

Is Oprah Winfrey a Listener?

While Oprah is most famous for her talk show, it was her ability to listen, and to find and develop common ground with so many different people, that allowed her to build the network and business empire that she has today. To excel at those skills one needs to be a strong active listener, something that articles about her recount in detail. She represents Listeners who successfully navigate through other people's suggestions and insights, taking feedback and counsel, and then making decisions about how to move forward. From her TV network to her magazine, she is able to bring ideas to reality.

Oprah is widely admired for the questions she asks and the empathy that she shows her guests, even while being direct. She knows how to ask tough questions, in part by restating what she thinks she's heard to inquire more deeply. As a result, Oprah's ability to connect with emotions and facts has allowed her to get highly sought after and exclusive interviews with influential people across celebrity status, whether they are politicians, sports figures, royalty, or otherwise. She is known worldwide for this community of friends and colleagues enabling her to be a household name. Listeners are known for their ability to cultivate relationships. They, like Oprah, have meaningful connections with others with whom they can discuss their decisions and thinking.

Chapter Six

The Thinker

Everything should be made as simple as possible,
but no simpler.
−Albert Einstein

You are a thoughtful decision maker, and you resist pressures to make rash decisions. You like to take your time weighing the options before moving forward, and you tend to look at all the possibilities, wanting to understand the positives and negatives of each decision choice. You don't necessarily need tons of data, like a Detective, but you do need the time and headspace to arrive at the best possible decision and feel like you have both a reason for the decision you're making and a rationale for why it makes sense. Speed is not your goal; process is.

Strengths

Being the Thinker means that you will not get caught off guard by the consequences of the decisions you make. You are thorough and thoughtful. You are cautious—you know what warning signs to look for, and you are good at steering yourself away from them. You're a master at making pro and con lists, or following other clearly established processes, and you rarely make decisions on impulse. This is a powerful strength because you know what you're up against. You're unlikely to be sold something that you don't want to buy because you rarely act without first considering all the angles.

Blind Spots

Being a Thinker can have its negatives too. Sometimes, because you are so cautious, you pick the safest option rather than the best option in order to avoid any chance of failing. This **loss aversion** means that you lose out on the opportunity to fail and learn from your mistakes: learning from failure has been shown to improve decision-making more than learning from success. Your aversion to loss even sometimes means that you choose not to make a decision rather than make one that might result in failure or loss. This nondecision is, of course, a decision—and one that can weigh on you and make you unhappy and uncomfortable. The result is that all decision-making can come to feel burdensome and weighty.

Thinkers can overthink decisions, which may cause them to get stuck, become paralyzed, and spiral into "analysis paralysis." A situation may be deemed too complicated, causing a potentially larger problem to arise. You're also not always popular with friends and family who want to be spontaneous because you're so uncomfortable with making decisions before thinking through the consequences.

Because you're a master at comparing and weighing your options, you sometimes don't weigh the value of each option individually. For example, option 1 may cost less than option 2, but if they are both under your budget, there's no need to eliminate the more expensive option. This **relativity bias** keeps you from seeing things as they actually are and inclines you to see them in comparison to something else. This flaw has a **frame blindness**, whereby decisions are influenced by the way information is presented. The framing effect may lead to a narrow view of a larger problem. And finally, because you are committed to identifying "tested" options, you tend to trust authority figures, assuming that they've done the testing work that you would do. This **authority bias** means that if someone you admire suggests a decision path, you'll give that choice more weight than perhaps you should.

Thinkers in Action

Michael's Example

Michael, a Thinker, is the CEO of a mental wellness start-up company with a software platform. Like all CEOs, he was facing a host of urgent decisions to make that seemingly all needed to be made at the same time. Michael and his staff wanted their site to provide safe and anonymous chat rooms where people could discuss a variety of mental health issues. However, Michael's team had come up with fifteen proposed mental health issues that seemed important and worthy of a chat room—including depression, anxiety, obsessive-compulsive behavior, and work-life balance.

Given that the company was still relatively young and had only a few corporate clients, his team felt strongly that it didn't make sense to launch all fifteen of the rooms at once. Without enough of an audience, opening too many chat rooms at once could lead to unused rooms, which would reflect poorly on the platform overall, making it less attractive and therefore less desirable. However, Michael could imagine reasons for many potential poor outcomes if his small company made the wrong choices. What if a user clicked on the chat room menu and saw a room for anxiety but not for depression? Would the site seem out of touch? Was it worse to have too few rooms or unused rooms?

Michael felt stuck. He was confronted with too many options and could see the downside of each; it was mentally draining. Each of the potential chat room topics felt equally important. How could he choose, for example, depression over anxiety? As a Thinker, he had always relied on a framework to work through decisions, but the framework that felt comfortable was a comparative one. Michael felt each option had to be weighed against each of the alternatives to select the best one, but this equivalency made an already difficult decision even tougher for him.

Michael decided to narrow the list down, but not as much as his team wanted. Instead of choosing four mental health topics to focus on as a start, as the team wanted, Michael narrowed the list down from fifteen to eight, double what was asked of him. The result was that his time-consuming "analysis paralysis" impacted both his leadership and the company. In the end, his team didn't feel they could push Michael to further narrow down the offerings because he felt so strongly that he'd thought the problem through carefully and completely. Michael moved forward with his hotel full of chat rooms—and the hotel is nowhere near full. Some of those rooms feel like parties nobody's attending.

Michael's paralysis was in part due to the fact that he only viewed his users from one perspective. He might have tried perspective-taking, looking at the problem from a variety of vantage points. Evidence shows that it is often easier to make a decision if you imagine helping someone else make that decision. How would you advise a friend facing the same situation? Then try your own advice.

Olga's Example

Thinker Olga is a stock analyst, with a focus on the auto sector and a solid track record recommending stocks for her company's clients. The job suits her strengths well. She is thoughtful and comfortable spending time dealing with both the details and trends impacting car companies. She studies their financial and investment performance, creates spreadsheets, and ranks the companies that she follows against one another. This frame of relative comparisons within a defined context is very comfortable for Olga (as it is for Thinkers in general) because she likes to understand the pros and cons of the options under consideration.

Olga is careful about her research process and doesn't like to give her final opinion about a company until she has completed her work. Sometimes this causes problems with her portfolio manager who wants updates immediately when market news occurs. He makes her feel rushed as she doesn't like to share her decisions until she's confident that she understands their implications and can clearly explain her reasoning to others. When she makes her recommendations she often lags behind her auto sector peers at other financial firms, but when she is comfortable delivering an assessment, her analyses are well thought out and focus on capital preservation to prevent losses to clients.

Because Olga's work focuses primarily on auto companies, she sometimes has a frame blindness about the industry. There may be times when investors would be better off avoiding auto companies entirely, but because Olga is always looking at the companies in comparison to each other, she has difficulty seeing when a "winning" company is really just the best player on a bad team, so to speak.

Thinkers like Olga would do well to recognize that although they excel at problem-solving, this is a different skill than excelling at decision-making. Solving a problem often includes an exploration of the issue or issues at hand, meaning that there is a process taking place. Making decisions, however, is an action. It may be an action alone, done without a process, or it can be based on and derived from the insights gathered during the problem-solving process. Problem-solving and decision-making go hand in hand but are not entirely the same.

If you are a Thinker facing a big decision, ask yourself, am I seeing the bigger picture that my problem fits into? Beyond identifying and evaluating the roots of an issue, what is necessary to set the decision-making into motion to address a problem in a timely way? What would give you the conviction to take action based on your analyses?

THREE TIPS FOR THINKERS

To avoid analysis paralysis, Thinkers can better identify a clear idea of what they want to achieve and what they are optimizing for in making their decisions so that it is easier to evaluate their options and remain within a time budget. We'll tackle how to focus on what you want from your decisions when we discuss Vision of Success later. But for now, a few tips for Thinkers to counter their tendency to overthink:

- Notice when you are stuck in your head. Overthinking can become such a habit that you don't even recognize when you're doing it. Start paying attention to the problem. Write down in a notebook or make a note in your calendar when you notice yourself overthinking so that you can begin to identify what tends to cause this behavior.
- Break the decision down. Are there small decisions that you can make more easily to help you make progress toward making a larger decision?
- Focus on the solution. Dwelling on your problems isn't helpful—but looking for solutions is. If it's something you have some control over, challenge yourself to consider how to prevent the problem or identify potential solutions. If it's something you have no control over—like a natural disaster—think about the strategies you can use to cope with it. Focus on the things you can control, like your attitude and effort.

Famous People with Thinker Attributes

Albert Einstein, scientist who developed the theory of relativity; Abraham Lincoln, sixteenth president of the United States; and Martin Luther King Jr., civil rights leader

Was Albert Einstein a Thinker?

Many people think that genius is the primary determinant of intellectual achievement. Yet one of the greatest Thinkers of all time, Albert Einstein, attributed his success not to his intelligence, but to his questioning mind. His curiosity and inquisitive drive enabled him to develop great questions that he then used to search for answers that redesigned our view of the physical world and the universe.

Was Abraham Lincoln a Thinker?

We can often spot a Thinker by looking for people who are cautious and thoughtful. History may not always present Lincoln as cautious and thoughtful, but he was. At the beginning of his presidency, even though he was anti-slavery, he did not publicly call for emancipation of slaves. He wanted to unify the nation, not divide it, so he stayed silent and didn't act on the issue until well into the Civil War. He represents one of the key strengths of a Thinker: the ability to resist the pressures to make rash decisions and actions, instead carefully considering the benefits and potential drawbacks of any option.

Lincoln also, like Thinkers generally, worked within the (political) system, looking at and comparing his options. Thinkers are realists who consider themselves to be pragmatic. When Lincoln saw that there was no hope of walking back from the ongoing Civil War, he updated his assessment of the political landscape, and this relative analysis of the situation finally gave him conviction to make his bold decision. In 1863—two years into the war—he (finally) issued the Emancipation Proclamation.

Was Martin Luther King Jr. a Thinker?

Although he was a revolutionary and charismatic leader of the civil rights movement, King was someone who always thought carefully and deeply about his actions. He wanted to work within the system. He struggled his whole life with how to change an unfair system from within. In his autobiography, he wrote about thinking through crafting his speeches to achieve this delicate balance: "How could I make a speech that would be militant enough to keep my people aroused to positive action and yet moderate enough to keep this fervor within controllable and Christian bounds? . . . What could I say to keep them courageous and prepared for positive action and yet devoid of hate and resentment? Could the militant and the moderate be combined in a single speech?"[1]

King also wrote about using the political system to effect change. In an article for the *Nation* that he wrote in 1961, he argued that the new president, John F. Kennedy, could use executive orders, enforcement powers, and presidential appointments to advance societal change. Who better to lead our nation's civil rights movement than a man who thoughtfully considered the long-term impact of short-term decisions? He carefully navigated through both the bad and the good in order to profoundly change the world.

Chapter Seven

The Visionary

Everything around you that you call life, was made up
by people that were no smarter than you.
—Steve Jobs

You don't like to settle for the ordinary, and you like to go your own way. When faced with any clear set of options, you're more interested in finding a different path, something that hasn't yet occurred to others. You keep every-one guessing—and often, you surprise those around you with your decisions!

Strengths

As a Visionary, your great strength is being able to see possibilities that other people may miss. When things seem too obvious, you get bored. You prefer to imagine and dream up new ways of doing things that no one has ever thought of. You are an innovator and an inventor. These traits make you a powerful decision maker because to you, the best option is the one you create yourself. The people around you admire what a strong individual you are. You aren't afraid to do what might be unpopular if you believe it will give you the best results. This also makes you a natural leader.

Blind Spots

Being the Visionary does have its drawbacks. You have a tendency to believe that with a creative spirit, you can accomplish anything. This can lead to **optimism bias** where you are overconfident in your judgment. It can also lead to being single-minded in pursuit of a goal, which to others can come across as valuing ideas over people and may cause conflict and hurt relationships. This single-mindedness sometimes combines with the **planning fallacy** where you think making and implementing a decision will take you less time to make than it does, leading to missed deadlines or other targets. In addition to miscalculating time, Visionaries may sometimes skip the planning process entirely, just assuming that whatever it is they envision, it will be possible.

With your preference for leaning on your imagination, rather than doing research, your opinions are sometimes shaped by limited information. Further, you can come across as a poor "team player" because you don't value or appreciate coworkers' ideas. With your propensity for being drawn to exciting ideas, you may fall prey to **saliency bias**, getting attached to the most recent or bold information or ideas, even if they aren't ultimately the most important. This saliency bias can lead you to make decisions based on a superficial understanding of the decision you're trying to make. Finally, because you like to go your own way, you sometimes try too hard to be an original. This tendency to overvalue originality because it's rare is a form of **scarcity bias**, devaluing things that are seen as common or plentiful. It can lead you to invest in being different as opposed to making the smartest decision.

Visionaries in Action

Jason's Example

Jason works for a consulting company and enjoys the constant variety of clients and content that his job entails. Every few weeks he's assigned to a new project, often in a new location or with a company in a different and new (to him) industry. As a Visionary he welcomes change. He also has no trouble coming up with innovative solutions to the challenges that the company's clients face, and he is comfortable bringing these solutions to his colleagues at the consulting company. But while he is working for a company of "problem solvers," his colleagues don't seem interested in new solutions. They rarely even want to entertain the options that he presents.

This makes him feel shut down and undervalued as part of the team. At the same time, his colleagues have expressed their frustration with Jason as a "team player." Jason's outside-the-box solutions indicate, to his colleagues, that he doesn't appreciate or understand that project workloads are demanding and time lines are tight. Jason's supervisor has even told him directly that they aren't interested in untested ideas; the company favors implementing solutions that have been successfully used in the past.

Jason wants to get along with his colleagues and better enjoy the way his job exposes him to a diversity of businesses and industries, but he realizes that he doesn't feel a sense of purpose at the consulting firm in part because he has little impact in his consultant role. He realizes that what is missing is a connection to a real feeling of contribution and a larger purpose, something that Visionaries especially crave.

Visionaries like Jason often have to consciously think about when and where they can air their ideas *and* have time to invest in them. Visionaries also benefit from considering that investing in relationships with as much gusto as generating ideas will make them seem more like team players— not always a natural inclination for such big-picture thinkers who also often want instant gratification and validation.

Andrew's Example

Andrew, who appeared in chapter 1, is the Visionary cofounder of a national education nonprofit focused on promoting positive school culture by building students' social and emotional skills. When he approached me about developing a decision-making program for high school students using the AREA Method, I agreed that, while it would be good to teach decision-making to young adults, my book, *Problem Solved*, and my work around decision-making weren't focused on the K–12 system. Andrew, like a true Visionary, listened to all the reasons why I wasn't a good fit for his program and pressed on, asking me to come to his office to discuss decision-making and the AREA Method in more detail.

When I arrived, I had no idea what to expect. I was ushered into a conference room with a giant blackboard. Scrawled on the blackboard in big letters was "BHAG: Every high schooler learns AREA and decision-making." I wasn't sure I understood what was going on, and I had no idea what the acronym BHAG stood for.

"BHAG?" Andrew said. "That's your Big Hairy Audacious Goal: to teach the world how to make inclusive decisions that combat bias and strengthen relationships."

As a Detective, I wasn't accustomed to having big, hairy, audacious goals. I'd mostly worked with companies, nonprofits, and college and graduate school students in business and journalism. And Andrew, while knowing the high school population well, had no experience in teaching decision-making either. Why did he take this on and take time from his day and mission to give me a dream that I didn't know was mine?

Still, with his encouragement and conviction that there was a real need for high schoolers to be more skilled in their decision-making, I began thinking about what it might look like to adapt my work and AREA Method for high schoolers. Even more, Andrew told me he didn't need me to solve the problem alone. He was so dedicated to realizing the potential of a program for young adults in decision-making that he met me where I was; he set me up with resources, opportunity, and authority to succeed by immediately staffing the project with two of his senior team leaders. Within weeks, a program took shape that was tested in front of a bunch of high schoolers—and on a Sunday no less! Andrew's infectious passion enabled him to enroll people for the large vision and to figure out the details.

Andrew's vision, optimism, and generosity have in part changed the direction of my own research and work. Our collaboration led me to create software—something I knew nothing about. I developed a series of decision-making modules that high schools across the country have adopted to help prepare young adults with decision-making skills.

Andrew's actions reflect a nuanced but significant difference between the Adventurer and the Visionary. Both archetypes have a lot of ideas, and both like to move fast. Both are optimistic, often fun, and also, at times, unrealistic. However, the Adventurer is committed to movement. Adventurers don't want to feel trapped. They like to make a decision as it comes up and then be done with it so that they can get to what's next. The

Visionary, however, is more committed to the idea than the movement. Visionaries don't always need to be the ones who carry out their big, hairy, audacious ideas even if they do want to see them born into the world.

THREE RECOMMENDATIONS FOR VISIONARIES

- Honor the other stakeholders in this decision. Remember that the way you see and experience the world is more expansive than most other people do. Of course, all PSPs need to be aware of the other stakeholders in a decision, but Visionaries in particular have a tendency to be so caught up in their vision that they forget that others might not see what they're seeing. And in order to make your vision a reality, you'll need to communicate it to others from their perspective, not yours. Consider how you can be someone that others want to listen to. Take the time to understand the viewpoints of others involved in this decision. If they can't hear you, they can't work with you to make your vision a reality.
- In your work with others, remember to provide a clear vision for the future. When you do share your ideas, get clear on the criteria for moving forward. How would the plan take shape? Are there specific steps you can identify? What might the deliverables be, and how do they align with the goals of your organization?
- Provide inspiration. Visionaries naturally push out energy that can invigorate but also drain others. To do more of the former and less of the latter, consider how you will prioritize your ideas to separate out when to move forward with an idea and when to ignore it. Being comfortable being honest with yourself as well as with others can make working with a Visionary a very rewarding experience.

Three Famous People with Visionary Traits

Beyoncé, the singer and entertainment icon; Steve Jobs, the entrepreneur and inventor who founded Apple and Pixar; and LeBron James, the NBA all-star

Is Beyoncé a Visionary?

Beyoncé is a legendary musician who continually stretches and changes what she's doing musically. She began her career as part of the group Destiny's Child and achieved great success. But instead of staying with what was comfortable, Beyoncé launched a solo career and made the recording industry work for what she saw as her goals.

Beyoncé thought that there needed to be a company for artists that melded both the creative and the business aspects of recording. In an interview with *Harper's Bazaar* magazine, she says, when she was twenty-seven, "I took control of my independence . . . and started Parkwood Entertainment. At the time, there wasn't a company that did what I needed it to do or ran the way I wanted it run. So, I created this multipurpose badass conglomerate that was a creative agency, record label, production company, and management company to produce and work on projects that meant the most to me. I wanted to manage myself and have a company that put art and creativity first."[1] In true Visionary form, Beyoncé didn't just see herself as a pop singer or even a superstar; she saw herself and her music as something bigger, as having the ability to change the world. And she is.

Was Steve Jobs a Visionary?

From the iPod, which held thousands of songs in your pocket, to Pixar, which transformed animation, Steve Jobs always went his own way. Like many Visionaries, Jobs was drawn to new ideas and unafraid to imagine possibilities well beyond what had already been done. From his days of building a Macintosh computer in his garage to launching his "Think Different" campaign, Jobs thrived when he was forging his own path forward.

However, Steve Jobs had some Visionary negatives too. He was known to set a goal and expect everyone to move in that direction. He became frustrated when people didn't "get it" because it seemed so obvious to him. Rather than clarifying goals and expectations, Jobs would publicly humiliate employees or just fire them outright. To avoid this pitfall, Visionaries will want to ensure that they make sure that others understand their goals and expectations and remember that success doesn't happen alone.

Moreover, Jobs was known to flout the rules (reportedly parking in handicapped spaces, for example) and make some very bad decisions. One was his decision to hire former PepsiCo chief John Sculley to run Apple. Feeling that he needed an experienced operating and marketing partner, the then twenty-nine-year-old Jobs lured Scully to Apple with the now legendary pitch: "Do you want to sell sugared water for the rest of your life? Or do you want to come with me and change the world?"[2] What a Visionary way to frame the decision!

Sculley took the bait, and within two years he had organized a board campaign to fire Jobs. While many people would have considered getting fired a failure, and Jobs told Stanford graduates in a speech that "it was awful-tasting medicine," the ever-Visionary Jobs didn't see it that way. "It turned out that getting fired from Apple was the best thing that could have ever happened to me. The heaviness of being successful was replaced by the lightness of being a beginner again, less sure about everything. It freed me to enter into one of the most creative periods of my life," he said. Visionaries don't need solid ground beneath them because they have confidence that they can create their own world.

What Makes LeBron James a Visionary?

As a twenty-three-year-old playing basketball for the Cleveland Cavaliers in 2006, LeBron led the league in scoring before he had anything close to an elite supporting cast, and he is still a wildly efficient, unstoppable finisher around the rim. He made the bold choice to be a free agent within the National Basketball Association, transferring from team to team, leading each to a national championship in their own right. Like most Visionaries, LeBron was less interested in the traditional and more interested in the exceptional. He has become a basketball legend not by playing by the preordained rules of the game but by crafting his own vision of how to play.

LeBron intentionally changes how he plays every few years. At different points in his career, he's been elite—if not the very best in the league—in virtually every facet of the game. In fact, he is so versatile that he can guard all five positions, and stories abound of his playing point guard and power forward on the same offensive possession.

In addition to his belief in himself, LeBron has a vision of the team he plays with, and he's not afraid to share this vision with his teammates to help uplift their game. When James returned to the Cavaliers, he was intent on bringing a championship to Cleveland, and he communicated that belief to his teammates. Sportscasters recount that before the season James gathered his teammates and told each player what he expected them to do. He let them know that he believed in them, that his vision for the whole team was achievable, and that helped boost their confidence that the Cavs could make that vision a reality.

Chapter Eight

Hunt Like the Cheetah

Without questions, experience and examples teach nothing.
—W. Edwards Deming

As I mentioned in the "How to Use This Book" section, the core of this book is the Cheetah Sheets, graphic organizers you can use and return to time and again as you work to be more mindful and dynamic in your decision-making. The questions in these sheets, named for the agile cheetah, are meant to be strategic stops, moments that temporarily slow you down to thwart bias and improve your analysis and efficacy.

The first Cheetah Sheet, Problem Solver Profiles, provides you with a synopsis of the different ways that people tend to approach problem-solving, and the strengths and blind spots of each approach. A blind spot, as defined by *Merriam-Webster's Collegiate Dictionary* eleventh edition, is a "portion of a field that cannot be seen" and may be "an area in which one fails to exercise judgment." Since all PSPs are associated with cognitive biases, those pesky mental mistakes that impede clear thinking, throughout this book, I'll use the term "blind spots" to refer to the cognitive biases collectively. Use this chart as a reference point once you begin to better understand your own approach or to consider the decision-making approaches of others. While this Cheetah Sheet is a touchstone as you begin the process of exploring Problem Solver Profiles, Cheetah Sheet 6, in chapter 10, expands on this initial overview to better explain the strengths and blind spots.

CHEETAH SHEET 1
Problem Solver Profiles

This chart provides you with a synopsis of the different ways that people tend to approach problem-solving. Refer to this chart to better understand your own approach or to consider the decision-making approaches of others. Cheetah Sheet 6: PSP Strengths and Blind Spots will expand on these PSP characteristics.

ARCHETYPES	STRENGTHS	BLIND SPOTS
Adventurer	Confidence Speed Efficiency	Optimism bias Planning bias Confirmation bias Closeness-communication bias
Detective	Committed to facts Rational Realistic	Confirmation bias Planning fallacy Projection bias Frame blindness
Listener	Trusting Relational Supportive	Authority bias Liking bias Narrative bias Social proof bias
Thinker	Thoroughness Thoughtfulness Caution	Loss aversion Relativity bias Authority bias Frame blindness
Visionary	Imaginative Innovative Individualistic	Optimism bias Saliency bias Scarcity bias Planning fallacy

Once you have a working familiarity with the broad strokes of each Problem Solver Profile, I suggest that you use Cheetah Sheet 2 to work through a self-reflection rear-view exercise about your PSP. It will help you examine some of your past decision-making through the lens of your new self-knowledge.

CHEETAH SHEET 2

PSP Decision Rear-View Mirror

This activity involves revisiting a past decision or interaction to examine and analyze it so that you may learn from the past and apply insights to future big decisions.

1. Think of a difficult or complex decision that you made in the past.

2. Write out the steps of your decision-making process.

3. What did you decide?

4. Do aspects of your decision-making align with your PSP profile?

5. Did you fall prey to any of the biases or blind spots associated with your PSP?

6. How has that decision worked out for you?

7. Looking at your PSP, can you identify what you might do differently if faced with a similar decision?

By writing your answers you'll encourage deeper introspection and improve your intuitive instincts to better harness your PSP knowledge. To help you, I've provided a model of a completed Cheetah Sheet 2 below. Warning: it may make you hungry!

COMPLETED CHEETAH SHEET 2

PSP Decision Rear-View Mirror. Niko's Example

Niko, the captain of a luxury cruise ship, learned that his PSP is the Detective. He uses this activity to revisit a past decision to examine how it aligns with what he's learned about his PSP's decision approach.

1. Think of a difficult or complex decision that you made in the past.
   As part of our cruises in the Caribbean we offer a weekly Beach BBQ to our guests. For the first BBQ of the season we were docking in a new island location. I turned to the checklist we'd always used for our beach BBQs and began to follow the steps. The first step was to buy lobsters for our guests.

2. Write out the steps of your decision-making process.
   I found local island fishery companies that would be familiar with the fishermen and market.

3. What did you decide?
   As soon as I reached a local company, I placed the lobster order by quantity, not specifying size of the lobster.

4. Do aspects of your decision-making align with your PSP profile?
   Yes, I followed the data, using the checklist. I also considered a local fishery as a knowledgeable agent, meaning that they had all the data necessary to do a good job.

5. Did you fall prey to any of the biases or blind spots associated with your PSP?
   Yes, I relied too much on the existing checklist and also made a series of assumptions. I thought dealing with this new supplier would be like dealing with the ones we've used in the past. I used the delivery date and number of lobsters as data and I ticked off the box "lobster" on the BBQ checklist as soon as we had our first offer. I also did not go back to consider problems we'd had in previous years, and I assumed that others were as familiar with the BBQ routine as I was.

   I assumed that a local fishery would know what to do for our lobster needs, but they didn't know our grill size, cook times, and plate size.

6. How has that decision worked out for you?
   We host around 400 guests and calculate half a lobster per person. Because the season had just started, we did not specify the size of the lobsters–normally we like 2lb lobsters. Offering half a lobster is our standard, it looks impressive on the plate and is enough to make anyone happy. We received lobsters that were 3lb to 5lb.

   The larger lobsters resulted in several problems: First, we ran into space issues on the BBQ. Second, the cook time was longer and therefore there were longer lines for guests. And third, the staff didn't know about cutting the lobsters in half and placing them on the guest's plate so instead placed the lobsters on the buffet for guests to take. No surprise, some guests walked off with two enormous whole lobsters on their plates. Our plates were literally too small. Overall, it was a disaster: long lines, some guests with no lobster, some guests upset for the wait. And on top of it, huge amounts of food waste.

7. Looking at your PSP, can you identify what you might do differently if faced with a similar decision?

In preparation for our next BBQ we sourced lobsters a day early on a different island directly from the fishermen. We specified size and number and made a seasonal agreement in which we accepted some larger ones as part of the deal. We also restructured the BBQ setup so that the chef served the guests directly from the grill. By making these adjustments we controlled the cost, secured supply for the season, enhanced our production efficiencies, were able to BBQ faster and avoid lines, and control the quantity served per person. Now when the chef puts one half-lobster on a plate hardly anyone asks for a second piece. Overall, we've enhanced the quality of the Beach BBQ experience.

In addition, with my Detective hat on, I made sure that every step of the Beach BBQ is now documented, and new procedures are made part of the operational guidebook. Instead of having some of the numbers, facts and procedures in my head, I now have them on paper.

Of course, many of the most important decisions that you make in your life are not made alone. The Problem Solver Profiles of those around you will impact your decision-making—and your comfort level with the outcomes of decisions.

How we make decisions isn't something that's taught in schools (yet) or discussed at team meetings or cocktail parties (yet). So how do you think about the Problem Solver Profiles of people around you? At times you'll be able to invite them to take the PSP quiz, whether they are a new colleague or a BFF. However, at times this valuable information may be something you want to derive on your own. For those times, below is a Cheetah Sheet to guide you to identifying and understanding the PSPs of those with whom you make your big decisions, whether they be family, friends, or colleagues.

CHEETAH SHEET 3
Identifying and Understanding Others' PSPs

This activity will help you identify and better understand the decision-making approach of those with whom you make your big decisions, whether they be family, friends, or colleagues.

1. Identify a situation or decision that the problem solver has made in the past. What seemed most crucial to them while making the decision?

2. What data collection techniques (or lack thereof) did the problem solver appear to use most often?

3. Using the PSP table, match their problem-solving strategy to Problem Solver Profiles.

4. Identify at least one other decision the problem solver has made. Did they use the same tools and techniques to make this other decision?

5. If the person did use the same tools, you can have some confidence that you're on the right track with a PSP identification.

6. If they made this other decision very differently, think about what other factors were at play: A personal versus professional decision? A different group of decision makers? An unfamiliar environment versus a familiar one? See the chapter on situationality and dynamic decision-making.

7. For the second decision, repeat steps 1–3. See the chapter on situationality and dynamic decision-making.

8. For the decision you need to make with this other person (or people), which past situation better fits the current decision you face? Using this information can help you understand how the other person may respond and allow you to temper your response to their response. The goal: to enter into problem-solving in a more inclusive and productive way.

9. If you are working with someone new and don't have a sense of their decision-making style, your work together can still be productive if you have a solid understanding of all the PSPs. Use the profiles to look for clues to what your new decision-making partner values—and to your response to that.

Below you'll see how Clara, an instructional coach, used this Cheetah Sheet to identify a colleague's PSP so she might challenge some of her assumptions to better explore solutions to a work problem. You'll read more about Clara in chapter 10: PSPs and Cognitive Biases.

COMPLETED CHEETAH SHEET 3
Identifying and Understanding Others' PSPs. Clara's Example

Clara, an instructional coach, who is a Listener, is working with Sam, a young teacher. Clara felt that her work with Sam wasn't as effective as it could be and was frustrated by this. So she began to think about what Sam's PSP might be. We'll be following Clara throughout the book. You'll meet her in more depth in chapter 10: PSPs and Cognitive Biases.

1. Identify a situation or decision that the problem solver has made in the past. What seemed most crucial to them while making the decision?
   I review some of my meeting notes from past sessions with Sam as well as a few of Sam's lesson plans. The lesson plans in particular reveal creativity and imagination. I realize that the originality of the lessons are important to Sam.

2. What data collection techniques (or lack thereof) did the problem solver appear to use most often?
   To me, Sam does not seem terribly focused on data. He often dreams up his ideas. When he uses data, he seems to value just a few salient pieces of information.

3. Using the PSP table, match their problem-solving strategy to Problem Solver Profiles.
   I think Sam is either an Adventurer or a Visionary. However, since my meeting notes record that Sam has been open to my suggestions and tends to take my advice, I think that he is more likely a Visionary. He values ideas.

4. Identify at least one other decision the problem solver has made. Did they use the same tools and techniques to make this other decision?
   Sam listens to his students' comments in class and is willing to be guided by learners' questions instead of classroom objectives.

5. If the person did use the same tools, you can have some confidence that you're on the right track with a PSP identification.
   Yes, I believe Sam is open to others and values ideas over details. Both decisions support my hypothesis that Sam is a Visionary. Knowing Sam's Visionary tendencies gives me enough information.

The next few chapters are focused on expanding your understanding of your PSP and how it plays out in your daily life, in different relationships, and in different environments. By exploring your past, you can begin to build a foundation to look deeply and critically at what you have done.

We'll first talk about risk because it is embedded in every decision, and we often don't recognize or acknowledge the role it plays. Next, we'll turn to cognitive biases, which can short-circuit a decision-making process, preventing us from mindfully making the best decision for the situation or ourselves. From there, we'll explore the difference between ambiguity and uncertainty, because understanding will enable you to craft a Vision of Success at the outset of your decision-making process. Once we've tackled this series of roadblocks, we'll focus on the different PSP strengths. The final chapters tackle the PSPs in the real world. What are the data traps that each PSP is vulnerable to? How do PSPs interact with each other and in different situations? Finally, we'll look at how to be a more dynamic decision maker. The goal: to help you build a better future with a decision-making roadmap that will bolster your strengths, limit your potential blind spots, and enable you to work better with other PSPs.

Chapter Nine

PSPs and Risk Profiles

It is not a calculated risk if you haven't calculated it.
−Naved Abdali

When I first started working with Ari on limiting child sex trafficking, I asked him about Protect Her Life's day-to-day operations. He told me, "We're in a constantly changing environment, requiring us to change our *entire strategy* every two to three weeks." The emphasis on "entire strategy" is mine. It was a startling answer—and so Visionary.

While it is useful to quickly detect new information and what is important and deserving of attentional resources, Ari was falling prey to salience bias. He allowed the new and prominent evidence to take precedence over—and cloud out—older or other data. Moreover, he was so confident in his assessment and analysis of the information that he was comfortable making big risky bets for the entire organization. His risk appetite—the amount and type of risk that Ari was prepared to pursue personally and for his organization—enabled him to make sweeping decisions advocating for quick systemic changes.

I asked Ari to elaborate, and he shared that "our attempts to plan workflows and measure milestones are often thwarted by the dynamism of the situation. Traditional project management methods seem ill-fitted for this project, so we're now trying to figure out how best to do it systematically."

His risk analysis of the child sex trafficking landscape in Ahmedabad caused him to define the problem that he needed to solve as one requiring that he look beyond "traditional project management." But had he identified the right problem?

Was Protect Her Life limited by existing organizational structures because of the complexity of sex trafficking itself? Or might the problem have been incorrectly defined? Might Ari's Visionary approach to decision-making, which values originality and is comfortable with risk-taking, have caused him to incorrectly identify what needed to be solved? When I asked him this question, it (temporarily) stopped him in his tracks. He said he had never thought about that before.

As a successful, thoughtful, and intelligent person, Ari assumed that he had correctly identified many of the elements needed to create an organization that could successfully tackle child sex trafficking. He had developed job functions for intelligence gathering, data analysis, "raid and rescue," and even aftercare for newly freed victims of trafficking. However, his own desire and draw to the new meant that he was not actually relying on those units to function independently. He also hadn't taken the time to think about how his small, new organization could be surgically effective; Ari's Visionary tendencies meant that he wanted to do everything—and all at once.

He hadn't recognized that his own approach to decision-making, and his biases, presented a risk to the organization that needed to be accounted for. He couldn't imagine that he wouldn't be effective, and that Protect Her Life wouldn't succeed or might even make the situation in Ahmedabad worse. He unknowingly approached the problem with what he valued personally and was potentially blind to a better or more accurate problem definition.

Like Ari, now that you've read about your Problem Solver Profile, and the profiles of other decision-making types, what can you do with the information? You can use the information and knowledge you have gained to examine your own decision-making tendencies—and those of others—in order to make your big decisions better. The first step is becoming more self-aware and learning to better understand why you feel what you feel and why you behave in a particular way.

How can this self-awareness help you? One of the very first takeaways is that each PSP thinks about risk—one of the biggest factors in decision-making—differently. So a first step to understanding—and improving—your decision-making approach is to understand your appetite for risk, your risk assessment patterns, and the risk analysis tools you rely on.

Ari didn't consciously think that he was framing decisions by optimizing for new and bold choices, but making this information explicit gave him the opportunity and freedom to do something different. It might be right for him personally to follow his instincts, but was it right as a leader of an organization, or did organizational success (particularly of a small and untested charity) depend in some part on stability and consistency?

Yes, Ari knew he was a bold thinker, and he liked being one; he knew that he leaned into creative solutions, and he saw that as a positive (which it often is). But the decision-making qualities that birthed Protect Her Life were not the same qualities necessary to create a sustainable organization. In fact, the constant shifting of goals was likely a destabilizing factor that undermined his leadership.

Ari couldn't recognize that a decision-making strategy that worked in one situation didn't work in all situations. This is true for all decision makers; our way of deciding doesn't work in every situation and doesn't work with every other decision maker. If you are a Detective, for example, working with an Adventurer, your individual risk preferences will be vastly different, and the problem that you think you are solving for (how to rein in the Adventurer) may not be the actual problem. This is situationality and community at work.

Having clarity about yourself and what you want can be empowering, giving you the confidence to make changes as you learn. Once Ari recognized and confronted his bias toward new and exciting ideas, he was able to begin doing the work to make his organization effective, stable, and well led. "We now have an organization-wide way of thinking that further fosters shared consciousness," he says.

If Ari's example feels too foreign (and let's face it, most of us won't start a Visionary charity in a foreign country), let's look at another example of a friend's patterns of decision-making that were circumscribed by her PSP's embedded risk tolerance, assessment, and analysis.

Lisa, a shy Detective, signed up for a dating app after a tumultuous divorce. Her children selected the app and created a profile for her with slightly tweaked biographical data, assuring her that privacy protections meant no one could download or search the posted photos. Knowing her children were far more acclimated to the world of social media, she took their assurances as reliable data.

Within twenty-four hours of posting her profile, Lisa received a message on LinkedIn from a man she did not know. He'd been able to identify her and gave her pointers about how to better protect her privacy. Lisa, concerned about safety, responded by immediately deleting her profile and the app. From her perspective, the whole experience was a fail. A single piece of data—that a stranger had been able to pierce the veiled identity and then track down her real contact information through the photos she posted—was proof to Lisa that a dating app was a terrible idea for her.

She recounted the story to her Thinker friend, Rhianna, and her Adventurer cousin, Stephanie. They both framed the problem differently. Rhianna's response was to remind Lisa that although she was going to meet many "wrong" suitors, all she needed was one "right" one—and a dating app might allow that one right suitor to find her. Stephanie saw Lisa's concern about privacy as overblown—and suggested replacing Lisa's professional headshot with less easily identifiable and more casual pictures. The headshot had been easily searchable but a snapshot from a friend's backyard barbeque would not be.

This story illustrates how different people think about a problem differently and assess risk differently. There are likely many times when your risk assessment is right for you: you may know, for example, that skydiving is a far too risky activity for you, and knowing exactly why you feel that way (and confronting it) doesn't matter. In fact, risk is often experienced as a visceral feeling, and those strong emotions give us information. But when we always allow ourselves to respond to that visceral risk response, we may be misunderstanding both the actual risk and our actual goals. This was exactly what happened to Lisa.

Even when we take the time to identify the risk in a decision, we may not include ourselves and our decision-making habits as being a risk.

So let's look at the components of risk: appetite, assessment, and analysis.

Risk appetite is the level of exposure you (or your organization) are willing to take. It is your tolerance for risk. It is subjective and will vary between and within PSPs. One Listener with a trusted group of advisors may have more risk appetite than a Listener who only has two good friends. Both, though, likely have less risk appetite than Adventurers, who are generally more comfortable taking chances in part because they value forward movement and are more optimistic about outcomes.

Once you've determined your risk appetite, risk assessment is the next step. Not all decision makers spend an equal amount of time on this step (and some may skip it completely). Risk assessment is about defining criteria to gauge if a decision is within your risk threshold. The Detective is naturally inclined to take this step because she relies on data and values research to get comfortable with a decision. The innovative Visionary, who enjoys risk-taking, may or may not bother to assess risk.

Risk analysis, the final step, comes when you are ready to analyze your results. Like risk appetite and assessment, risk analysis is also subjective; different PSPs will look to different analytical tools. Those tools portray different pictures of their data and provide different kinds of insight. For example, the Thinker, who tunes into her inner voice, likes to feel that she has fully understood the consequences of making a decision. In contrast, a Listener, who relies on getting outside counsel, may allow other voices to replace her own, and therefore incorrectly assess and analyze the risk she faces and the problem she is solving for.

In my books, *Problem Solved* and *Investing in Financial Research*, I lay out different analysis tools as part of the AREA Method to assist you in this step. If you are a decision maker who hasn't thought explicitly about how you analyze risk, I encourage you to read through the Exploitation chapter of both books for some specific risk-analysis tools and their benefits and limitations.

Let's look at each PSP's relationship with risk when shopping for a new car after noticing that a neighbor just got a Tesla:

- The Adventurer, bored with her Volvo station wagon, sees the neighbor's Tesla and thinks how much more interesting it is than her car. Yes, she has two more years of driving her son—and his equipment—to hockey practice, but when she looks online, she discovers that the Tesla has an enormous trunk. The trunk and the fact that it comes in a pretty blue are all she needs to move forward. She is comfortable with risk and decisive.
- The Detective, already in the market for a new car, likes the look of the neighbor's Tesla, but her risk appetite is much lower than the Adventurer's. Before even going online, she reads up on reviews from *Consumer Reports* and analyzes what charging an electric car may do to her electric bill. Only after this research does the Detective even visit the Tesla website—where she discovers that the lease terms are quite favorable.
- The Listener also wants to assess and calculate risk. When she sees the neighbor with the cool Tesla, she rings the neighbor's doorbell, asks her how it drives and what she thinks of the car, its price, and so on. But the Listener wants more information. She calls customer service and talks to the salesman, bringing that information back to her partner for more discussion. At her book group, she mentions her interest in Teslas, and she later calls her dad. Her assessment of risk relies on others' understanding.
- The Thinker sees the cool Tesla and wonders about the cost-to-benefit ratio of a purely electric car. She looks at other electric vehicle options and compares them to hybrid options as well.

The Thinker actively works to reduce risk in her decision-making by evaluating a range of options. But this can lead to a cycle of decision-making where the primary decision doesn't get made because she begins to consider secondary decisions, such as whether adequate charging stations will be available for a yearly trip upstate.

- The Visionary, looking at the neighbor's Tesla, is drawn to its newness and originality. Concerned about the impact of gasoline-powered cars on the environment, she wants to be at the vanguard of clean energy cars. Drawn in by the vision of a "better" car, she doesn't assess whether the Tesla is truly the best car for her. She is confident in her ability to finance the purchase. It satisfies her preference for taking risks that support her larger goals.

What you'll notice from the above car purchase decision is that each of the PSPs bridges the relationship between biases and decision risk differently. Adventurers are comfortable with risk. Detectives may assess specific aspects of risk. Listeners tend to assess risk based on other people's perspectives. Thinkers may consider primary and secondary consequences of risk. Visionaries may optimize for a risk that suits a larger purpose.

Below you'll find two Cheetah Sheets dealing with the PSPs' risk profiles and what it means for their decision-making. The first Cheetah Sheet contains a table that outlines the different ways that the five PSPs frame and break down the three elements of risk that make up risk tolerance: appetite, assessment, and analysis. It also contains a question for each PSP to consider to control for and counter issues that may result in an incorrect assessment of risk. You'll notice that PSPs vary across the three elements of risk. For example, while an Adventurer has a healthy risk appetite, he or she may not value assessing or analyzing risk. However, a Listener with a lower risk appetite puts a higher value on risk assessment and analysis. The variance between risk outlook and these different risk elements makes plain why decision-making may be so thorny between different PSPs and why bringing this knowledge to bear before making decisions with others improves decision-making ease and satisfaction while strengthening relationships.

The second Cheetah Sheet has guiding questions with recommendations for you and your organization to consider aligning along a risk profile so you may better navigate your big decisions with others.

CHEETAH SHEET 4

PSPs + Risk

Use this table to analyze the different ways that the five PSPs frame and break down the three elements of risk: appetite, assessment, and analysis. The terms "high, medium, and low" refer to the value each PSP applies to that aspect of risk. Apply the questions in the Considerations column to each PSP to check and challenge how you and others are navigating risk.

PSP	RISK APPETITE	RISK ASSESSMENT	RISK ANALYSIS	CONSIDERATIONS
Adventurer	**High** Favors making a lot of decisions (quantity).	**Low** May not assess the risks she faces in detail because she can always make another decision.	**Low** Doesn't invest in consistent risk analysis.	Are you navigating a hurdle or making a decision? Simply moving forward is not the same as problem solving.
Detective	**Low** Enjoys researching a decision but may miss out on the emotional aspect of the decision.	**Medium** Risk can be assessed against data, but if there is not enough data or the "right" data, a Detective can get stuck.	**High** Does the analysis of the assessment support the decision?	Have you tuned into the emotional aspects of the decision? Are you allowing data collection to drive your problem-solving without assessing what you're really solving for?
Listener	**Varies** Favors relying on others to make a decision. Willing to take significant risks with consensus.	**Low** Relies on others to define risk criteria, which may or may not reflect the Listener's own criteria.	**Medium** By relying on others, a Listener may end up with a decision that's not right for her.	Is the way others understand your problem aligned with your values and needs? Prior to asking for input from others, identify your own Vision of Success. (See chapter 11 for more on VoS.)

PSP	RISK APPETITE	RISK ASSESSMENT	RISK ANALYSIS	CONSIDERATIONS
Thinker	**Medium** Is concerned with understanding the risk calculation.	**High** Confident in her own ability to assess and compare risks between options—if she believes that she's gathered enough data.	**High** Can cycle into "analysis paralysis."	Are you protecting the downside more than the upside? Intentionally consider what could go right when conducting your analysis.
Visionary	**High** Committed to pursuing dreams.	**Low** More committed to the vision than realities.	**Middle** May or may not analyze the risks, but the risk is not as salient as the potential reward.	What tethers success to reality? Consider what cost of failure you are willing to accept.

Once you understand your risk profile, you can begin to bring that knowledge to personal and professional decision-making by considering how others think about and navigate risk. By assessing risk tolerance both for ourselves and for others we are working with, we strengthen our relationships and decisions.

CHEETAH SHEET 5
PSP + Risk Alignment

Use this activity for you and your organization to consider aligning along a risk profile so you may navigate your big decisions better.

1. For any major decision, start by looking at the chart in Cheetah Sheet 4: PSPs and Risk. Read across for the risk profile for your dominant PSP. Reflect on the strengths and potential blind spots enmeshed in your decision approach. Ask yourself the question in the column labeled Consideration.

2. Ask yourself: Is your personal risk preference right for this decision and this group of decision makers or organization? In Ari's case, his personal risk preference was not a good fit with his organization's needs. As a Visionary, he is comfortable with risk and equates it with opportunity. But that wasn't right for Protect Her Life, which needed more stability.

3. Using your understanding of your colleagues' or fellow decision makers' PSPs, assess their risk preference and whether it is a good fit for the decision and the organization. You may be able to do this with your team. If not, to do this for others, look back at Cheetah Sheet 3: Identifying and Understanding Others' PSPs.

4. With the other decision makers, discuss the group's level of risk appetite. Having a common definition and lexicon helps everyone feel included and understood and lays a foundation for a more fulfilling discussion and problem-solving experience.

5. Write out a risk appetite statement that everyone can agree on. Make it clear that the statement is not just a topic of conversation, but rather is something that you and your team or family are committing to. Consider:
   • What kinds of risk-taking do you want to encourage?
   • What kinds of risk-taking do you want to prevent?
   • How can you continuously assess and analyze risk?

6. Risk assessment: After deciding what your risk appetite is, how will you assess the risks of the situation you are evaluating? At its core, assessing risk is about defining objective criteria that you can vet with research.

> 7. Risk analysis: In this final step, you are ready to analyze your results. Keep in mind that risk analysis is another subjective step and that different analysis tools will result in different pictures of your data and provide different kinds of insight. Consider a risk analysis tool that will best reflect the assessment criteria you've selected.

Having a risk statement that explains how you and your team define and manage risk sets the guardrails not just for a single decision but for decisions going forward.

For example, Tony was in charge of his company's flagship annual conference. Due to an impending blizzard, the company was forced to consider suddenly canceling their conference. Tony knew that there would be all kinds of fallout from canceling. How should he manage the fallout to be in line with his company's values, purpose, and goals? The company faced losing out on sponsorships and key potential new business contacts, disappointing the program planners, and paying a forfeiture fee to the venue, to name a few consequences.

It's easy to get caught up in the immediate problem, but in defining risk appetite, Tony needed to think about focusing on what matters most to the company before dealing with the problem itself: What did they want to preserve? What did they hope to encourage and to protect: already established professional relationships, the monies at stake, or the new contacts? Defining the company's risk appetite enabled Tony and his team to weigh what may seem like competing concerns (the lost dollars versus the future business relationships).

Below is Tony's Cheetah Sheet that he used to consider his own risk preference and align with his team on what was best for his company.

COMPLETED CHEETAH SHEET 5
PSPs + Risk Alignment. Tony's Example

Tony, a Thinker, is a senior manager at a global company, faced with deciding whether to recommend that his company suddenly cancel its flagship conference. He uses the Cheetah Sheet: PSPs and Risk to first identify his PSP's risk preferences; second, to assess its applicability to his decision; and third, to sync up with his team to create a shared risk profile for the decision.

1. For any major decision, start by looking at the chart in Cheetah Sheet 4: PSPs and Risk. Read across for the risk profile for your dominant PSP. Reflect on the strengths and potential blind spots enmeshed in your decision approach. Ask yourself the question in the column labeled Consideration.
I read the Thinker risk profile and decided to make a list of what could go wrong by canceling the upcoming conference and a list of what could go right from what I perceive is my company's perspective.

2. Ask yourself: Is your personal risk preference right for this decision and this group of decision makers or organization? In Ari's case, his personal risk preference was not a good fit with his organization's needs. As a Visionary, he is comfortable with risk and equates it with opportunity. But that wasn't right for Protect Her Life, which needed more stability.
I think my cautious Thinker approach might be well suited to considering the downsides of canceling the conference, but am I framing the problem too narrowly? And there are some risks I just don't feel that I have a good handle on. In reading about my PSP's biases I want to make sure to challenge the Thinker's loss aversion and frame blindness.

3. Using your understanding of your colleagues' or fellow decision makers' PSPs, assess their risk preference and whether it is a good fit for the decision and the organization. You may be able to do this with your team. If not, to do this for others, look back at Cheetah Sheet 3: Identifying and Understanding Others' PSPs.
Based on my personal experience with each of my team members, when I reviewed the PSP chart, I think my sales manager is a Listener. The head of the marketing team is a Visionary. In reading next about their risk profiles, I think my Listener sales manager may be most concerned with the client relationships and may only focus on that, which is not a full picture of the decision risk. For my marketing chief, the Visionary might focus on the company's image and how to creatively spin the opportunity and present the conference content. For me, I want to make sure the Visionary marketing chief sees and accounts for the downsides of cancellation. I now have a better handle on the PSPs on my team. I'm ready to bring the group together to look first at our own decision-making styles and what they foreground and background for this decision.

4. With the other decision makers, discuss the level of risk appetite for the group. Having a common definition and lexicon helps everyone feel included and understood and lays a foundation for a more fulfilling discussion and problem-solving experience.

   Write out a risk appetite statement that everyone can agree on. Make it clear that the statement is not just a topic of conversation, but rather is something that you and your team are committing to. Consider:

   - What kinds of risk-taking do you want to encourage?
     We are willing to risk incurring loss, inconveniencing people, and interrupting business temporarily to follow safety guidelines.
   - What kinds of risk-taking do you want to prevent?
     We want to prevent damaging new and existing business relationships and our reputation.
   - How can you continuously assess and analyze risk?
     Risk can be assessed and analyzed by speaking with stakeholders about their goals for the conference and developing other ways to deliver conference content and networking opportunities to meet those priorities.

   COMPLETE RISK APPETITE STATEMENT:
   While we are willing to risk incurring financial loss, inconveniencing people, and interrupting business temporarily to follow safety guidelines, we will mitigate our risk of losing business and hurting our reputation by speaking with stakeholders about their goals for the conference and discussing other ways to deliver conference content and networking opportunities to meet those priorities.

5. Risk assessment: After deciding what your risk appetite is, how will you assess the risks of the situation you are evaluating? At its core, assessing risk is about defining objective criteria that you can vet with research.
   I used the team's risk appetite statement to define objective criteria by highlighting important phrases that are actionable in the risk appetite statement:
   While we are willing to risk incurring financial loss, inconveniencing people, and interrupting business temporarily to follow safety guidelines, we will mitigate our risk of losing business and hurting our reputation by speaking with stakeholders about their goals for the conference and discussing other ways to deliver conference content and provide networking opportunities to meet those priorities.

I use the bolded phrases to build out the questions that my company needs to answer:

- **Loss:** How much money will we lose by canceling?
- **Inconveniencing people:** What kinds of losses will clients/customers/attendees incur? How much will those potential losses be?
- **Interrupting business:** Comparative analysis of other similar cancellations and their fallout?
- **Speaking with stakeholders:** Which ones? How to frame the conversation and identify their perspective and priorities?
- **Other ways to deliver conference content:** What are the options? Where, when, and how might delivery occur? How do the options meet stakeholder priorities?
- **Provide networking opportunities:** What are the options? Where, when, and how might delivery occur? How do the options meet stakeholder priorities?

6. Risk analysis: In this final step, you are ready to analyze your results. Risk analysis is another subjective step because different analysis tools will result in different pictures of your data and provide different kinds of insight.
   While there are many good analysis tools, my team selected a pre-mortem to strength test the decision to cancel the flagship conference. We imagined that the decision "failed" so that we could examine what might go wrong after the cancellation. This helped us identify and shore up weaknesses in the plan to give the decision a better chance to succeed.

We can never fully eradicate risk—and most of us would not want to. Putting money in the stock market is a risk—yet it is also the best vehicle for most Americans to save for retirement. When we book a vacation to a tropical island or adopt a puppy from the local shelter or buy a used car on craigslist, we are taking risks. By recognizing that different PSPs think about risk differently, we can make our implicit risk tolerances explicit—and thereby improve our decision-making. Nearly five hundred years ago, Swiss physician and chemist Paracelsus expressed the basic principle of toxicology: the dose makes the poison. The risk of our decisions depends on a variety of factors, including ourselves: *How much risk are we comfortable exposing ourselves to, and what does that mean for how we expose, impact, and work with others?*

Chapter Ten

PSPs and Cognitive Biases

The difficulty lies not so much in developing new ideas,
as in escaping from old ones.
−John Maynard Keynes

In one of my monthly calls with Ari, he shared that he and his team were preparing an awesome thank-you gift for their donors: it would be a beautiful book filled with impressive bells and whistles, stories, and photographs, with a sumptuous leather cover to complete the keepsake. Ari's Visionary tendency to fall prey to salience bias meant that once he'd begun thinking about this book, he focused on it to the exclusion of other elements of his job and his year-end to-do list. In fact, he kept thinking of new elements to add to the book so that it began taking an incredible amount of his and the charity's time and resources—just as the planning fallacy would predict.

I asked Ari if the book would include data about the charity's impact on the ground. Ari hadn't focused on the data, however, because collating data felt so small and uninteresting next to the soaring narrative and emotional impact of a book filled with photographs and personal stories of girls who were rescued from sex trafficking. Ari's Visionary bias to see and overvalue the unique—scarcity bias—blinded him to what might most matter to donors: the quantified impact of their donations. He was so taken with the grandness of what he was doing that he missed the power and value of the "boring details."

Knowing his Visionary tendencies, Ari shared with me an incredibly detailed spreadsheet of the book that was being created for the donors and the materials it was being made from. He knew he needed the feedback of someone who made decisions differently. I congratulated him on wanting to do something "Visionary." He wanted an emotional response (which is also so Visionary!) but I suggested that his charity needed a more pragmatic one.

As a Detective, I'm inclined to dig for the boring (but important) details. I felt badly that I was lighting a match to Ari's beautiful Visionary book idea, but I also knew that Ari needed to reframe the goal of this "thank-you" project on the unit economics of his charity, on how his charity achieves those outcomes, and on where there was leverage in the charity's business model to expand its work and impact. As the CEO of Protect Her Life, Ari didn't need an emotional response from his donors; he needed continued financial support. The personal stories were of course not irrelevant, but Ari needed a strong economic story that shared the impact of dollars invested.

The point is that knowing your PSP doesn't automatically mean that you're going to make better decisions or be able to compensate for your biases and blind spots. However, the knowledge gives you the opportunity to begin the hard work of escaping from your old ideas. More specifically, it gives you the chance to challenge the comfortable decision-making strategies relied on in the past. We may think we're seeing—and making decisions—clearly, but in reality, we're too often peering through our dirty windshield of cognitive bias, layers of past experience, habit, and emotion that have stuck to us in ways that we may not recognize.

Like Ari, you may have also noticed that your decision-making strengths can sometimes be weaknesses. You may not have sat down and thought about them in an organized way, but now that you've met yourself through your Problem Solver Profile, it's the perfect opportunity to get better acquainted with your weaknesses as well as your strengths.

Yes, you'll want to read about the cognitive biases that you are most likely to fall prey to, but be sure to read all of the other PSP biases (see Cheetah Sheet 1: Problem Solver Profiles). Biases affect lexicon, situationality, and community just as the Problem Solver Profiles themselves do.

Situationality is extremely important when understanding how you—or those around you—may fall prey to certain biases because these biases can impact your relationships. You may not see that someone is falling prey to a bias—or that you are—because it is a bias not associated with your dominant PSP. Think about where and how situationality may lead you to make decisions differently.

For example, my mother is a pediatrician, and when she is at work she approaches her decision-making as a Thinker, exploring all possible options before settling on a preferred path forward. However, when my mother is with her family, she is very blunt. She goes with her gut and shares what she thinks—like an Adventurer. This has led to some fun moments of laughter. But it also can be hurtful and shocking, as when my oldest daughter excitedly modeled her purple prom dress and Mom said it looked simply awful. Her optimism bias lets Mom think that she can say whatever she wants in the context of a loving family relationship and her words will be heard with love.

It took me a very long time to recognize that Mom, like all of us, made decisions differently in different arenas for a few reasons. First, I hadn't considered situationality and how confusing that can be; Mom makes "Dr. Mom" decisions very differently than "Family Mom." Second, even when I began exploring the different ways people make decisions, I was working in the context of strengthening others' decision-making skills. I wasn't focused on stepping back and thinking about myself—and my family—as decision makers. So Mom and I would end up in the same patterns of decision-making conflict over and over again.

At some point it would have been wise to stop asking Mom's opinion on my kids' clothing choices for special occasions. Frankly, I don't know why I didn't prime Mom that we were sharing my daughter's excitement about her purple prom dress, which we'd *already bought*. Perhaps it has to do with my Detective framework; I was confident that my big girl and I had looked at all the dress options and selected the best one. My confirmation bias may have clouded out my ability to recognize that Adventurer Mom might see and understand the options differently.

Even when I had the lexicon for decision-making styles, it didn't occur to me to think about my family through that lens. My PSP work was part of my professional life, and Mom is my personal life. Ironically, I kept expecting Mom to react with her family in the same way as she reacts with her patients.

So even though I found Mom's attitude cavalier and at times thoughtless, it didn't occur to me to think about her Problem Solver Profiles. Not understanding where she was coming from, my responses to her were reactive, not proactive, and, frankly, didn't help the situation. However, as soon as I applied the Problem Solver Profiles to Mom, I began to see her behavior and actions in a completely different light—and I was able to see that her PSP was situational, and radically different in different situations. Suddenly Mom's actions no longer seemed episodic and random. She was clearly a Thinker professionally, but with the family, Mom's approach followed a different yet quite consistent pattern. It was a huge revelation for me to realize that Mom, with her family, is an Adventurer.

Understanding both situationality and lexicon, I've been able to improve and better enjoy my relationship with Mom, which is the third component: community. Recently, when I realized that I didn't know any of my parents' computer passwords and wanted to inquire whether they had an organized system for keeping and sharing this important information with one another, I didn't bring it up when Mom popped over to visit. A project like cataloging passwords is just the kind of thing that Adventurer Mom would hate and immediately reject. So I applied my newfound understanding of Mom's biases and instead wrote a short email. This would mean she wouldn't immediately reject it face to face and would give her some time to think through before responding. In addition, I included my dad in the email because Dad is a Detective and would slow down Mom's shoot-from-the-hip response.

In the chart below, you'll find a handy synopsis of the Problem Solver Profile strengths and blind spots. Both strengths and blind spots, or weaknesses, play into each profile's cognitive biases. Read over the chart.

CHEETAH SHEET 6
PSPs Strengths + Blind Spots

Use this table as an expanded synopsis of Cheetah Sheet 1: Problem Solver Profile strengths and blind spots to better understand how cognitive biases positively and negatively impact each PSP.

PSP	STRENGTHS	BLIND SPOTS
Adventurer	**Confidence:** You believe in yourself. **Speed:** You move quickly to make decisions. **Efficiency:** You can get a lot done in a short period of time.	**Optimism bias:** You're confident that decisions will work out well. **Planning fallacy:** You think everything will happen more quickly than it does. **Confirmation bias:** You focus on new information that confirms your beliefs. **Closeness-communication bias:** You overestimate the effectiveness of communication when engaging with someone who is considered close.
Detective	**Committed to learning:** You like to be well informed. **Rational:** You don't like to let emotions distract you. **Realistic:** You like to be down to earth and practical.	**Confirmation bias:** You focus on new information that confirms your beliefs. **Planning fallacy:** You think everything will happen more efficiently than it does. **Projection bias:** You assume your personal preferences will remain the same over time. **Frame blindness:** You misunderstand a problem and options based on information presentation and availability.
Listener	**Trusting:** You tend to believe in the people around you. **Relational:** You tend to build and keep friendships. **Supportive:** You tend to support others.	**Authority bias:** You give more weight to the opinions of authority figures and experts than others. **Liking bias:** You overlook the faults of, and comply with, wishes of well-liked others. **Narrative bias:** You make sense of the world through stories. **Social proof bias:** You adopt the actions of others in an attempt to reflect correct	behavior in a given situation.

PSP	STRENGTHS	BLIND SPOTS
Thinker	**Thoroughness:** You like to think things through. **Thoughtfulness:** You like to consider all options. **Caution:** You like to be careful and measured.	**Loss aversion:** You prefer to avoid losses rather than to acquire equivalent gains: you're more focused on not losing $5 than on finding $5. **Relativity bias:** You make relative rather than absolute evaluations. **Authority bias:** You give more weight to the opinions of authority figures and experts than others. **Frame blindness:** You misunderstand a problem and options based on information presentation and availability.
Visionary	**Imaginative:** You tend to have creative ideas. **Innovative:** You tend to introduce new concepts or thinking. **Individualistic:** You tend to think and do things your own way.	**Optimism bias:** You are optimistic that decisions will work out well. **Saliency bias:** You use available traits to make a judgment about a person or a situation. **Scarcity bias:** You overvalue things in limited supply, high demand. **Planning fallacy:** You think everything will happen more efficiently than it does.

Let's look at the PSP biases in action.

Say it is the end of the year and in addition to holiday shopping and celebration, you want to make sure you get those end-of-year charitable donations done. You're getting emails from charities you've donated to in the past. You're also passing Santa ringing his bell by the supermarket. You're getting snail-mail charity flyers from some charities you've heard of and some you haven't, the *New York Times* is running daily articles about the Neediest Cases Fund, and over dinner with your folks, they tell you that they've added more food pantries to their donations list this year. Think first about how you respond to these various stimuli. How do you make decisions related to your charitable donations?

If you take a look at the Problem Solver Profile Strengths + Blind Spots chart above, you can begin to see that different decision makers will approach this situation differently. Look at the decision-maker descriptions below and see if you can match each to the PSP, and identify which specific strength or bias that may be at work:

- Kai wants to think outside the box in his donations, searching for new charities or organizations and tackling some under-the-radar problem such as providing for bail bond charities.
- Robert is enamored by the new trend of community refrigerators and wants to buy out the vegetables at his local grocery store and fill them up.
- Ava read an article in the newspaper about the good work of a domestic violence charity and then checked the organization out on Charity Navigator, comparing it to other domestic violence organizations. She also thought about whether it might be more effective to give money to a shelter or an advocacy organization.
- Maxwell wanted to donate to a food pantry but was unsure whether to donate to a local group or a national one. He researched how much national food pantries were spending on their overhead and called several local food pantries to ask about their overhead costs. How many people were they able to help? What were their funding sources? He wanted to ensure that he chose a charity where the bulk of funds would go toward helping people.

- Maeve asked her parents and some of her close friends where they were donating, and added charities based on the recommendations of people she trusted.

You can check how well you matched the PSP to each decision-making approach:

1. Kai: Visionary. Visionaries value novelty and bold ideas, but this scarcity bias may also make them less inclined to donate to more well-known and proven charities.
2. Robert: Adventurer. Adventurers are confident and open to change. They might easily adopt a new idea, but this optimism bias might cause them to overlook information that might disconfirm their ideas.
3. Ava: Thinker. Thinkers want to know that they're making thoughtful decisions, but their careful approach can also lead them to a relativity bias, and they can end up overthinking or analyzing possibilities, making it hard for them to come to a final decision.
4. Maxwell: Detective. Detectives are comfortable conducting research to support their decisions, and while many good decisions are made with data, Detectives can overdo it and end up going down a rabbit hole and falling prey to planning fallacy. This slows down their decision-making as they continually search for more data.
5. Maeve: Listener. Listeners are good at finding out information from other people, but that same strength can lead them to fall prey to social proof bias, where they may allow the voices of others to drown out their own preferences.

The truth is, however you choose to donate, you're taking a positive step to help others in need.

Still, the questions above demonstrate that there are clearly different approaches to decision-making, and that all of them have unique and different strengths and weaknesses. Deciding how to distribute your charitable giving is a low-stakes decision with a high return. But there are other higher-stakes decisions where the decision-making approach and biases may impede your ability to move forward comfortably into your unpre-dictable future.

Four Scenarios: PSPs and Cognitive Biases in Action

Below you will find four relationship scenarios that we frequently find ourselves in: peer to peer, hierarchies from the vantage point of a leader, hierarchies from the vantage point of being subordinate, and in a team environment. Each anecdote shows you how the PSPs interact and how they may misalign and/or misunderstand one another. Although this chapter is focused on weaknesses (biases, assumption, and judgment), it is never possible to truly separate your decision-making strengths and weak-nesses. They are always two sides of one coin; a strength in one situation can be a weakness at another point. What's more, our biases can often lead us to see another PSP's strengths as weaknesses.

So, as you'll see in the scenarios below, both biases and strengths are always at work; we are never just our strengths or just our weaknesses—and the same is true for the other stakeholders in any decision. In the upcoming chapters, we will revisit these four relationships to focus more directly on both motivation and strength. Learning about your PSP is a "strand process," and it isn't always possible to separate the strands completely.

Now let's meet our four sets of problem solvers.

Peer to Peer

Saadia and Kavita
Detective/Visionary

A recent example with big consequences highlights how two different peo-ple approached a work-related problem. Their different Problem Solver Profiles, and related cognitive biases, negatively impacted both people and each of their companies' bottom lines.

Saadia, a professional writer, was approached by an acquaintance, Kavita, about contributing to a new project that Kavita was launch-ing. It would provide women with leadership coaching, a cause dear to

Saadia's heart. The two acquaintances had several phone calls where Kavita outlined her vision for her software platform and asked for Saadia's help with three things: coaching, running workshops, and providing website content. Saadia found Kavita's enthusiasm and energy to be infectious, and she loved the idea of working on a project that supported women's professional development. Saadia drew up a contract and, knowing it was a start-up, put in several protections to limit her downside risk.

The contract was signed and the project got underway. Saadia and her team blocked out their work schedules to ensure that her small company could deliver the services that were agreed to. Saadia met each self-imposed deadline and shared her progress with Kavita in phone calls and emails.

Then, the day before the second month's deliverable was due, Kavita called Saadia to say that the entire project would need to be paused; she didn't have the funds available to pay Saadia for the past month's work. Saadia was dumbstruck by the phone call and unsure of how to respond. She had her own staff to pay and had counted on the revenue for her own business's health.

Of course, this looks like a situation with poor communication, and it is. But understanding the PSPs of the two professionals and their related biases can shed light on why the communication was so lacking. Moreover, it can illuminate why taking into account self-knowledge about your own decision-making approach and taking the time to better understand the PSPs of other stakeholders involved in your decisions may improve both your relationships and decision quality.

As a Detective, Saadia had leaned into her data-driven worldview, where both projection bias and confirmation bias got in her way. She assumed—and projected—that her attention to details and careful planning was a behavior pattern shared by Kavita. She further "confirmed" this assumption when Kavita included Saadia on a call with her entire executive team—all seasoned professionals who headed up the company's technology, marketing, and strategy. Saadia, struck by the level of experience the team had, inferred that this was a sophisticated (and therefore well-funded) operation.

How might things have gone differently? While hindsight is 20/20, in the moment, you can put your PSP to work for you, even when you need to map the other person's PSP. Here's how it might play out: Saadia could have begun by thinking through her initial, pre-contract interactions with Kavita. What did she know of Kavita's professional journey? She might have found that Kavita held a variety of jobs, which, according to LinkedIn, included stints as deputy mayor in her hometown, running a podcast about innovation, and launching a nonprofit to help stray cats. That would have revealed some of Kavita's Adventurer and Visionary tendencies.

Coupling the professional background with what Saadia knew about the team Kavita assembled at her start-up might have led her to settle on more of a Visionary profile. Where an Adventurer might try to go it alone, a Visionary would be more likely to shore up her weaknesses by surrounding herself with a team of domain experts—as Kavita had done. Saadia assumed that all of this expertise meant that Kavita's start-up was a well-bankrolled company. Instead of asking Kavita for specifics about how the tiny start-up was financed, Saadia substituted assumption for knowledge—and made assumptions based on how she would have acted.

If Saadia had begun the partnership discussions looking for PSP clues, it may have alerted her to some common Visionary blind spots: optimism bias and scarcity bias. Could Saadia have probed for both? Certainly, writing downside protections into their business contract showed she was concerned about working with a start-up. As a Detective, however, who believes facts matter and sees a contract as agreed-upon facts for guiding future actions and responses, Saadia never thought that Kavita would disregard a signed contract.

Optimism bias might have been visible if Detective Saadia wasn't so focused on how to deliver everything that Kavita was asking for. Saadia saw herself as obligated by the facts of the contract. Stopping to think about PSPs, she might have wondered how such a tiny start-up could be doing so much all at once. Kavita, possibly operating under the Visionary's scarcity bias, may have wanted to lock up Saadia's time and talents, with her optimism bias leading her to believe she could work out the details of payment later.

Saadia didn't lean into what she knew—what was right there—because she was blinded by her own cognitive biases. Her Detective PSP focused on the data points: new business, a new market, cash flow, and growth for her own company. She immediately began with the "how" to make it happen. Where a Visionary saw possibility, Saadia's Detective felt a lack of follow-through and professionalism: different sides of the same coin (or the many coins Saadia is out now).

Hierarchy–Subordinate

Calvin and Talia
Listener/Thinker

Moving from a peer-to-peer example to one with a hierarchy where our decision maker is the junior member, let's meet Calvin, a Listener, who is employed as a junior designer at a well-established, brand-name global company. He is relatively new and has been staffed on a variety of projects, each one composed of teams of people with whom he needs to interact. Calvin is not shy about asking questions to better understand details, goals, and deliverables.

At year-end, Calvin prepares his self-review for his manager, Talia. He presents her with a write-up of how he has supported each project team's members. He focuses his write-up on what each team accomplished. He is surprised when Talia sends it back to him quickly, asking for more hard facts to quantify his accomplishments, wanting to know, "specifically, but what have you done?" Calvin feels hurt and misunderstood.

Here Calvin could have used both his Listener PSP strengths and potential blind spots to guide his review. His PSP strengths match him well. He is trusting, believing in his colleagues and his company's mission. He is also relational and supportive.

The flip sides of these coins are also blind spots for Calvin: liking bias, social proof bias, and narrative bias all clouded his ability to give himself a clear pat on the back. He wanted to show that he was a team player, focused on the company's goals, so he shared his accomplishments through stories instead of details and numbers.

If he'd been focused on his PSP knowledge, he might have set himself up for better success. He might have used his weekly calls with Talia in two ways: to check his own potential blind spots and to assess her PSP. Calvin could have asked about what constitutes success for a year-end review, and even for a sample of one that his manager considered to be well done and why. This may have shown him that he needed to specify his individual achievements related to the projects he'd worked on.

Paying attention to clues about his manager's PSP, Calvin could have tuned in to how often Talia expressed wanting to take a cautious approach to a decision, and he might also have observed her keen interest in knowing all her options. Calvin might then have pegged Talia as a Thinker. Tuning into Talia's Thinker tendencies, Calvin might have checked which strengths and potential blind spots could frame the Thinker's decision-making approach, noticing that relativity bias and authority bias could be important.

Relativity bias focuses on relative comparisons. For a year-end review, that might have tipped Calvin to be more assertive about the specifics of what he actually did, what deliverables he was responsible for on each project team, and how he completed those tasks.

For authority bias, he might have also gotten to the same result, being more focused on outputs than inputs. He might have considered what his performance means for Talia. Namely, Talia would need to share with *her* manager how she had performed with managing Calvin. She needed Calvin's specific successes and failures spelled out.

Both Calvin and Talia have different priorities; Calvin prioritizes collegial relationships while for Talia accountability is a top priority, both as a Thinker who likes to be able to explain decisions to herself and as a manager who needs to report up. Calvin's and Talia's differing priorities are not inconsistent. But if Calvin can apply the language of Problem Solver Profiles and his understanding of the situation Talia faces as his manager, he can be far more successful in his work relationship with Talia.

Group Dynamic

Avonelle, Dad, and Brother
Detective/Adventurer/Thinker

This next scenario involves a group dynamic in a very personal context: gathering at the holidays amid the pandemic. Avonelle, a young professional in her thirties, is a Detective. Her family wants her to travel the ten hours back to Georgia for Christmas. Her brother and her father all live in Georgia—although in different parts of the state. The goal: a family holiday celebration.

Avonelle, ever the Detective, reads COVID-19 updates in the news, listens to a science podcast on her morning dog walks, and reaches out to her ICU nurse friend for on-the-ground, real-time information. Knowing the cumbersome quarantine rules and process, she feels like she has enough information to make safe travel plans for herself but is concerned that her family won't have gathered all of the data she has. Avonelle takes the initiative and creates a safe COVID plan for everyone, which she proudly shares on the next family Zoom call. It's a disaster and everyone feels put out.

Given Avonelle's worry that her family would view the risks differently, how might focusing on her PSP and related strengths and biases have helped with communication and perspective-taking?

First, Avonelle's love of data made her assume that everyone else would be equally swayed by data. She only saw the situation from her own perspective. Second, if she'd considered the other PSPs, it would have helped her see how to make her argument more effective. Her family were not strangers. She'd had years of interactions with them and could have taken the time to apply the PSP framework to her thinking about her family long ago.

For example, her brother is usually a rule follower, but he likes to weigh his pros and cons before making a decision. Knowing this, Avonelle might have pinned him as a Thinker who likes to explore his options. She could have recognized that he doesn't want a decision handed to him; he needs to consider the options for himself. Dad is always an optimist who just wants Avonelle home and is confident that they can figure out the details once she arrives. If Avonelle had tuned into Dad's optimism, she might have seen that he's likely an Adventurer, willing to take risks and confident that he can deal with whatever comes up. For Dad, lots of details are a turnoff, and numbers, while an important piece of the puzzle, are not the only answer. Too much data frustrates him because he thinks it doesn't capture the big picture.

Knowing this, Avonelle might have spoken to her dad's planning bias and explained that *not* having a plan in place was both too optimistic and dangerous. With an unknown like COVID, they couldn't just assume that all would go well. Avonelle could have connected to Dad emotionally, speaking more of an Adventurer's language, expressing her worry that she might be asymptomatic but could transmit the virus to her much older father, and she couldn't take that risk. She could not visit without a plan.

Hierarchy–Leadership

Clara and Sam
Listener/Visionary

Our last example is a high school instructional coach working with a young, relatively new teacher. Clara, a Listener, meets each Thursday afternoon with Sam, a creative and energetic young science teacher popular with students and faculty alike. Clara prepares for each meeting by observing one of Sam's classes each week to identify areas that he can improve, reviewing Sam's lesson plans for one class for the week, and reviewing previous meeting notes. Clara has noticed that while Sam was often resistant to incorporating her ideas initially, he is beginning to take her advice and is now better matching his content to the amount of time he has to teach it. He's also improving at regularly checking that his students are following and understanding the lessons.

But Sam is often late to his meetings with Clara, even though the meetings are scheduled to be during his period off so that they can spend a full hour together. Often, and without warning, Sam shows up ten minutes late. Clara has asked him about it and gotten noncommittal answers. When she's offered to move the meeting time or date, Sam demurred. Yet his chronic lateness makes Clara feel disrespected and frustrated. She has put serious time and effort into preparing for the meeting. Clara knows that she needs to tell Sam that he must show up on time for their meetings to work, but she's uncomfortable being so direct and harsh.

From Clara's perspective, Sam is chronically late and unapologetic about it: how dare he waste her time. However, when Clara, as a Listener, looks at her own biases and blind spots, she realizes that she is subject to liking bias. She wants Sam to like her, so she's been reluctant to share her expectations for meeting times clearly and directly with Sam. She recognizes that what feels obvious to her may be too gentle and oblique for Sam.

So how about Sam's possible PSP? With his creative and energetic approach to lesson planning and teaching, and the fact that he bristles at or deflects Clara's suggestions for improvement, Sam seems to have Visionary qualities. Sam loves to create lessons that are unique, valuing originality over the tried and true, which suggests that he falls prey to scarcity bias, common among Visionaries. Sam also often can't get his lessons completed in the time allotted, which suggests an Optimism Bias, also a frequent blind spot for Visionaries. By seeing him as a Visionary, Clara realizes that Sam has a different view of "ten minutes late"; he's not deliberately disrespecting her, he just has his eyes on a different prize. She checks her assumptions with evidence by using Cheetah Sheet 3: Identifying and Understanding Others' PSPs.

A few ways these two PSPs can work better together to overcome their clashing styles: as a Listener, Clara has several choices. It isn't comfortable for her to lay down the law; it's not her style. Her experience of Sam leads her to believe that it wouldn't be received well either. She decides instead to focus on Sam's desire to be the captain of his own ship: she will turn the decision over to him as to whether they meet for fifty minutes or an hour. If Sam feels he benefits from the hour, then he may be willing to shift his behavior. For Clara, this strategy also feels more comfortable because she doesn't have to be "the bad guy," and it allows her to listen to how he thinks about the time they spend together. She makes the offer without emotion so she doesn't come across as taking over the process, using her Listener strengths of being relational and trusting so Sam will know she's genuine in her offer.

What the four scenarios illustrate is that when we are in a decision-making situation with someone else, and in particular someone else we don't know well—not our spouse of thirty years but a new client we are wooing—we view conflict around decision-making through the lens of our strengths and the other person's weaknesses. This is about recognizing *your* biases and also identifying and reframing the other decision maker's weaknesses as strengths.

Although the chapter is about cognitive biases, there is no way to look at blind spots without looking at strengths. They are two sides of the same coin. In the following chapters, we'll explore the facets of this coin—but it's all the same coin.

So the next time you face a big decision, take a Cheetah Pause, strategically stop, and remember that your perspective of a scenario may not be the whole story. Taking the time to pause and be deliberate now will ultimately speed up your efficacy. Below is a Cheetah Sheet for limiting biases. We'll build on the work you'll do in the below Cheetah Sheet when we turn to bolstering your PSP strengths in chapter 12. After the Cheetah Sheet, I've provided Clara's story mapped as answers below each question so you can see how the template might work and how Clara used this distance and reflection to provide space and strategy to decide how to best move forward with Sam.

CHEETAH SHEET 7
Limiting Biases

Use this activity to put Cheetah Sheet 6: Strengths + Blind Spots to work to limit your biases. Keep your answers handy to use to bolster your PSP strengths when we explore Cheetah Sheet 9: PSP Strategies to Bolster Strengths + Limit Biases.

1. List your PSP strengths at work in this decision you are faced with.

2. Reframe each of your strengths as potential pitfalls or biases. For example, if you pride yourself on your rationality, you may come across to others as cold and distant.

3. Think: how might those weaknesses be coming across to the other stakeholders? If you, thinking you're being rational, appear cold and distant, other stakeholders will be afraid to express their feelings because you are not expressing yours.

4. For your other stakeholders, what are you seeing as their weaknesses and biases? Again use Cheetah Sheet 6 to review Strengths + Blind Spots.

5. Reframe each of the other stakeholders' weaknesses as strengths. For example, someone who seems "flighty" might be considered "creative" and someone who is "late" could also be "always willing to make time to help a colleague."

6. With your new perspective of PSP strengths and blind spots, what is your understanding of the decision problem now?

Below is Clara's exercise.

For Clara, a Listener, she prides herself on connection by listening to others. She's been frustrated by Sam's chronic lateness and wants to solve the problem and strengthen the relationship.

COMPLETED CHEETAH SHEET 7
Limiting Biases. Clara's Example

Clara, an instructional coach, who is a Listener, is working with Sam, a young teacher. Clara felt that her work with Sam wasn't as effective as it could be and was frustrated by this. She uses Cheetah Sheet 7: Limiting Biases to examine where she may be making assumptions and judgments.

1. List your PSP strengths at work in this decision you are faced with.
   As a Listener, I see myself as relational, trusting, and supportive.

2. Reframe each of your strengths as potential pitfalls or biases. For example, if you pride yourself on your rationality, you may come across to others as cold and distant.
   a. **I realize that my desire for connection means that I work to avoid any whiff of conflict.**
   b. **I realize that what I see as trusting is an assumption that Sam values the same things I do. His values may not be mine.**
   c. **I realize that what I see as supportiveness can come across as controlling to others. I want to meet for an hour because, as a Listener, I value in-person contact. I realize that other PSPs might feel supported (and be supportive) without needing so much in-person time.**

3. Think: how might those weaknesses be coming across to the other stakeholders?
   a. **I realize that because I prioritize being relational and connected I may have successfully hidden from Sam my perception that there is a problem with Sam's lateness.**
   b. **I realize that I trust Sam to prioritize what I value but I haven't discussed those values, which in this instance means being on time. I haven't asked Sam what he values; perhaps he values our time together so much that he needs a few minutes to switch from his teacher head to being a student himself?**
   c. **I realize that I have no idea what Sam considers to be supportive. Perhaps he feels very supported by the time and content that we explore together.**

4. For your other stakeholders, what are you seeing as their weaknesses and biases? Again use Cheetah Sheet 6 to review Strengths + Blind Spots.
   I see Sam as flighty, unreliable, and disorganized.

5. Reframe each of the other stakeholders' weaknesses as strengths. For example, someone who seems "flighty" might be considered "creative" and someone who is "late" could also be "always willing to make time to help a colleague."

   I realized that Sam's flightiness is because he is enthusiastic and creative, always thinking ahead about new, exciting lessons.

   Perhaps Sam's lack of reliability is because he truly is busy and often responding to student needs after class.

   Perhaps Sam's disorganization may not be disorganized to him; it may be a different kind of organization. He may have papers everywhere, but he can always find what he needs—eventually. Sam is more focused on ideas than on whether he's filed away his old lesson plans.

6. With your new perspective of PSP strengths and blind spots, what is your understanding of the decision problem now?

   Based on completing the Cheetah Sheet activity, I realize that "disrespect" is not at play. The exercise helped depersonalize the problem. I feel a sense of relief and more positively toward Sam. I realize now that the decision we need to make together is about how to use our session time.

Taking the time to slow down and create this deliberate disruption may seem unnatural—and it is. But like the cheetah's hunt, which benefits from strategic stops to boost agility and flexibility, it's work that provides so much in terms of improved decision-making. It aids communication, efficiency, and effectiveness for any working relationship.

Each Problem Solver Profile has a language all its own. But they need not be foreign languages to us; we can learn them and then speak them.

Chapter Eleven

Ambiguity versus Uncertainty

Values are like fingerprints. Nobody's are the same,
but you leave 'em all over everything you do.
—Elvis Presley

Ari envisioned creating an organization that would stop child sex trafficking completely. But how? With money he had raised from another Visionary project (a behavioral psychology conference), Ari flew to India and hired private investigators who could help him begin to understand how child sex trafficking worked. The investigators quickly began to identify trafficking victims and locations, and Ari's nonprofit, Protect Her Life, began raiding sites and rescuing girls and women.

But rescuing victims wasn't going to solve the larger problem of sex trafficking. With the investigators' help, Ari identified seven important components that were necessary to truly end sex trafficking: identifying and disrupting sex trafficking pipelines; locating red-light districts and other private locations used for sex work; rescuing trafficked children and women; providing police with the proper training and information so that they could work to bring down sex traffickers; providing safe houses for rescued girls and women; providing all the necessary components to rehabilitate the rescued victims; and assisting prosecutors by both preparing witnesses and supplying evidence. In true Visionary fashion, Ari was so moved by the importance of the work that he wanted to do it all.

That's where Ari and his organization were when I began working with him. He'd had some important—and emotionally resonant—successes with his scattershot approach. There was no question that he had changed lives. But he hadn't created a sustainable organization with a clear mission, vision, and game plan for change. He had emotional stories and a daring rescue to share, but he didn't have a coherent story; he was spending money on everything—because it all felt important. He hadn't developed priorities or a master plan that would pay for everything.

Since Ari wanted to do everything, his organization was doing everything. Ari had a vision, but he hadn't stopped to think about how he and the organization could truly accomplish their mission and fulfill that vision. Ari could see the big picture in his mind, and he could put many pieces in place, but he had no blueprint for how to turn his beautiful big picture into a sustainable, focused, effective plan and organization.

Working with Ari, I guided him to take a step back. What was his organization really about? What was their value proposition? I asked him to take the time to think about what really mattered most. As the leader of a small charity, he needed to prioritize. He liked learning the stories of the women and children that Protect Her Life had saved, and he loved sharing these. But while they were moving and helped bring in some donations, stories alone weren't enough.

The work that Ari and I had done to first identify his PSP and then explicitly assess the Visionary's embedded risk tendencies and review associated biases prepared us to now more easily identify what he valued for his organization. For while the truth was that there were many ways Ari could have made an impact on reducing sex trafficking in India and any one of them could have been successful, he, and his charity, could not be successful if they spread themselves too thin. Another charity might choose a different path and be effective. But in order for Ari to feel successful and effective, he needed to first figure out what he valued: he needed to know what would feel like success *for him*.

Ari was uncertain about the best way to move forward with Protect Her Life because there were so many possible paths. However, the right answer for Ari was *not* uncertain; it was ambiguous. In other words, it was a judgment call and a matter of interpretation. The path forward needed to be guided by data, but the data could be interpreted and used in many ways. How it would be used by Ari and for Protect Her Life was personal for them and needed to be aligned with their values and their mission. This is where ambiguity comes in.

Ambiguous situations are those situations where the best outcome *is* a matter of interpretation. Gathering more data will never resolve ambiguity.

It couldn't tell Ari which direction Protect Her Life should go all in on. His decision—and yours—will ultimately be a judgment call.

A judgment call based on values is a judgment call that you can feel good about because you are being led by what matters to you. But how do we drill down on what matters to each of us, or to our family, or to our organization? And how does the practice bolster our PSP strengths to confront an ambiguous problem? The AREA Method has an easy-to-use answer for this: invert your problem solving. Instead of focusing on the problem itself, define what a successful outcome looks like—what I call your "Vision of Success."

Vision of Success is one of the core principles of the AREA decision-making system, which I laid out in my books *Problem Solved* and *Investing in Financial Research*. It acknowledges that one of the thorniest parts of complex problem-solving is how to get started. And the best way to get started is to connect with your values, which can guide you to a result that is successful for you personally or professionally.

How do you connect with your values? And how do you use them for direction? Values are our North Stars. But we sometimes lose track of them. However, the truth is that while values may be ambiguous, they are rarely uncertain.

Your values are likely linked to your Problem Solver Profile, your risk preferences, the biases you fall prey to, and your strengths as a thinker and decision maker. Honing in directly on what you value and believe can guide you through your (unpredictable) future. Your values provide personal boundaries and a path forward. Tuning into your values allows you to work toward a future that aligns with your vision of a successful life.

We each have an inner voice that speaks to us. Sometimes it speaks from fear and loss, and you may want to challenge that voice; but often it speaks from a place of love and connection, and you want to honor it. Knowing your values allows you to hear that inner voice.

Take the example of parents trying to figure out how to raise successful, well-adjusted children. Every parent at some point has asked themselves the question, *How do I raise good kids?* We all navigate that question with some uncertainty—we can research child development or listen to the advice of experts—but research and data won't provide a step-by-step path forward for each parent and family because ultimately the definition of a "good kid" is ambiguous. One parent might feel a "good kid" is a child who's academically successful while another feels it's one who's emotionally close to her family. Or who's physically active and a good team player. Or who's a creative thinker, unafraid to march to his own drum. For each parent and family, the answer will be different, but when the definition, and the choices a family makes, are guided by the family's values, the answer will be the right one—for that family.

The same is true for organizations. For example, Eric Dawson, a Visionary (as many charity founders are), created Peace First to empower young adults to promote peace. His charity operates today in 140 countries. In 2018 Peace First was awarded a small grant from the Gates Foundation to explore expanding their work into the Middle East and North Africa, the so-called MENA region. Peace First had no idea whether young people in the region would be open to and engaged by peacemaking work. Through the grant, they found the answer: yes. But as the grant was ending, the organization arrived at a "choice point," Dawson says. "Without the grant, should we wind things down in the MENA region, or keep our presence small, or scale up slowly, or place one of our two or three big bets in this area?"

As a Visionary, Dawson of course wanted to stay in the MENA region because it was a place of such conflict that making a difference there felt important. Succeeding there appealed to Dawson's Visionary desire to solve an intractable problem. It would really change the world. But he had gotten to a point as a leader that he knew to put guardrails around his Visionary tendencies. Each pathway forward had a myriad of issues connected to it that could put the organization's future at risk. Dawson knew that he couldn't make the decision on gut alone. He needed to differentiate between his personal values and the organization's values.

Dawson and Peace First looked to their mission statement—which outlined the organization's values—to define their vision of success. Ultimately, they decided that their existing work was fundamental, and any new opportunity—even a glorious one that showed great promise—could not be allowed to detract from existing projects. Once they were grounded in what success looked like—maintaining their presence and impact in the 140 countries where they were well established—Peace First could assess the fit of the MENA project. From there, the charity evaluated and decided that yes, the MENA-area opportunity met Peace First's mission, impact, and fundraising needs. They elected to continue working in the region but did not make a bigger investment in this new project and did not divert resources that might risk the other good work they were doing in the world.

Like Dawson, Ari needed to tune in to his Visionary strengths and biases to get to his core values so that he could plan for a sustainable future for Protect Her Life, one with measurable outcomes. We began by inverting Ari's problem and starting at the end. I asked him: What has to happen for you to know Protect Her Life is a success? Ari knew that he wanted to be able to say that fewer girls and women had been pressured into sex trafficking.

How would Ari define "pressured into sex trafficking"? Ari saw that pressure as coming from criminal networks who profited from stealing or buying girls and turning them into sex workers. My next question, then, was "What can you do about that?" Despite how moved Ari had been by each of the stories of the women and children his organization had rescued, he recognized that rescuing one person or even many people wasn't going to do anything to disrupt the criminal networks he believed needed to be stopped. He began to tune in to what would really matter to him: systemic change.

This was a huge revelation. It meant that Protect Her Life's focus needed to be on the criminal networks of traffickers and *not* on the victims. Each daring rescue provided a rush, which Ari, as a Visionary, loved. But those rescues weren't doing much of anything to change the future; all they did was change the real estate. Identifying and removing some of the middlemen in sex trafficking rings would have a much larger impact than identifying and arresting madams or pimps in a brothel, who were at the end of the chain: strategically removing a link in the middle weakens the entire chain.

This focus on Ari's values entirely changed and redirected the charity's goals and resource allocation. Now, with the "what" and "why" of his organization better defined, Ari could interpret how that values-based Vision of Success could be carried out; what was the plan that would work toward that success?

Starting from your values allows you to make a plan that will help you plot a path through ambiguity. Whether you are planning for your family's or your organization's future, values alone are not a road map, but they are a starting point and are often aligned with your PSP's strengths. A Visionary who wants to be original, as Ari did with his determination to stop sex trafficking, may value differentiation more than a Listener, who may be guided more by a desire to achieve community and connection.

Two people facing the same decision may choose very different paths forward because even if they are looking at the same information, how they value and interpret that information will likely differ. So there's nothing wrong with making a plan based on your values, even as others would make a different plan.

Once you have clarity on your values and your own Vision of Success (VoS), you're ready to create a personal road map to that success. How? By deriving your Critical Concepts—the one, two, or three things that you will need to deeply and creatively investigate in order to achieve your Vision of Success. The good news is that the Vision of Success has in it the seeds of your Critical Concepts: generally, it's the noun phrases that appear in your VoS.

For Ari and Protect Her Life, the VoS read as follows:

Protect Her Life will be successful when the criminal networks that perpetrate child sex trafficking incur substantive damage.

The noun phrases are in bold below (note that Ari added to the end of his VoS as we worked together and you may too. It often takes a few renditions to clarify your own thoughts, and that is what writing is; writing *is* thinking):

*Protect Her Life will be successful when **the criminal networks** that perpetrate **child sex trafficking** incur **substantive damage** through **legal means**.*

What do the noun phrases mean? This is where you can clearly see that the answers are ambiguous. You and I might define these terms differently. For Protect Her Life, turning the noun phrases into thesis statements that are researchable laid out the route to achieving Ari's Vision of Success:

- **Criminal networks:** We will map out the criminal networks and understand who and what is involved.
- **Child sex trafficking:** We will map out and understand where, how, and why children under eighteen are brought into sex work.
- **Substantive damage:** We will map out and understand the most effective ways to inflict real, lasting damage on criminal networks.
- **Legal means:** We will connect with police, politicians, and the legal system to amplify our efforts.

By identifying his and his organization's Critical Concepts, Ari created an actionable plan from a big-picture vision that was rooted in his values.

CHEETAH SHEET 8
Using Inversion to Derive Your Vision of Success

Use this activity to help you navigate ambiguity by identifying your decision's success metrics rooted in your values.

1. Begin to focus on your end goal by inverting your problem and answering the two Vision of Success questions:
   a. What has to happen in the outcome of your decision for you to know the decision was successful?
   b. Who else is involved in this decision, and what does success look like for them? (You might have to ask them this question directly.)
2. Combine your answers to A and B above to draft a Vision of Success Statement.
3. Highlight the nouns/noun phrases in your Vision of Success Statement.
4. Use the noun phrases to derive your Critical Concepts. Those factors will need to be made more specific.
5. Craft one or two researchable thesis statements for each Critical Concept. Finding the evidence to back up your researchable statements will move your decision problem from where you are to achieving your Vision of Success.

Here's an example of how Ariana, a Listener and a wealth manager at a global investment bank, and her team used inversion to derive their Vision of Success and identify their Critical Concepts to decide how to pitch their business to a prospective client.

COMPLETED CHEETAH SHEET 8

Using Inversion to Derive Your Vision of Success. Ariana's Example

Ariana, a Listener, is a wealth manager at a global financial company. She is bidding on a new client's business. She uses Cheetah Sheet 8 to navigate ambiguity to identify a Vision of Success and Critical Concepts for the pitch.

1. Begin to focus on your end goal by inverting your problem and answering the two Vision of Success questions:
   a. What has to happen in the outcome of my decision for me to know the decision was successful?
   My team and I wrote that we need to "Meet client's goals and convince client this company is best suited to meet her long-term investment needs."
   b. Who else is involved in this decision, and what does success look like for them? (You might have to ask them this question directly.)
   Having met with the client and spoken to her about her goals, we wrote, "Client has a short time frame to make her decision, has complex financial needs, and is looking for a long-term relationship with a full-service financial planner."

2. Combine your answers to A and B above to draft a Vision of Success Statement.
   We work quickly to demonstrate that our company offers unique and superior services that will specifically address the client's complex needs and desires while building trust in order to develop a long-term relationship.

3. Highlight the nouns/noun phrases in your Vision of Success Statement.
   We work quickly to demonstrate that our company offers unique and superior services that will specifically address the client's complex needs and desires while building trust in order to develop a long-term relationship.

4. Use the noun phrases to derive your Critical Concepts. Those factors will need to be made more specific.
   1. **Our company**
   2. **Unique and superior services**
   3. **Complex needs and desires**
   4. **Trust**
   5. **Long-term relationship**

5. Craft one or two researchable thesis statements for each Critical Concept. Finding the evidence to back up your researchable statements will move your decision problem from where you are to achieving your Vision of Success.

CRITICAL CONCEPTS:

1. **Our company:** We define our company through our unique and superior services, our ability to understand and meet the client's complex financial needs, our trustworthiness, and our history of stable, long-term client relationships.
2. **Unique and superior services:** We demonstrate that the company's core competencies meet the client's needs and are unique.
3. **Complex needs and desires:** We can demonstrate to the client that we understand her complex financial situation and goals.
4. **Trust:** We demonstrate the relationship aspects that the client values.
5. **Long-term relationship:** We demonstrate that we have a history of long-term client focused relationships.

Now that you've made the noun phrases specific and clear, you know how to translate your main ideas into what you need to research and understand in order to realize your Vision of Success. Moreover, you and your other stakeholders are in sync and aligned now.

Chapter Twelve

Using PSPs to Bolster Strengths

There are two ways of exerting one's strength:
one is pushing down, the other is pulling up.
–Booker T. Washington

Although Ari came to me for guidance because he wanted help turning his beautiful brainchild of a charity into something that could make lasting change, Ari had incredible strengths as a Visionary. As mentioned earlier, on the plane home from his initial trip to India, while he was still a Costco executive, he read a book about British intelligence actions during World War II. His creative thinking led him to see that a story of British intelligence could be a template for the anti–sex trafficking charity he wanted to create. Then, with only a sketch of an idea for Protect Her Life, he quit his (safe, secure, well-paying) job—and convinced his college roommate, Tim, to do the same (it helped that Tim is also a Visionary). Using their Visionary passions, Ari then created a funding source for the initial work of the charity: a behavioral science conference that he and Tim organized out of thin air in just a few short weeks.

The truth is, like Ari, we all have strengths as problem solvers and thinkers, and it is as important to work from—and honor—those strengths as it is to work against our biases and shortcomings.

Being in touch with our values helps us understand how we judge people and situations. Identifying our own values gives us important information about ourselves and can also give us insight into our own thinking and assumptions. For example, honesty is paramount for Saadia, the executive coach and writer, so when Kavita, who was starting a women's leadership website, was unable to meet her contractual obligations, Saadia immediately labeled the behavior as dishonest.

However, by identifying honesty as *her* key value, Saadia was able to step back and ask herself whether "dishonesty" was an appropriate label for what really happened. There was no mention of an intention to mislead.

Knowing that Kavita values bold creativity, her admission that she couldn't pay Saadia and needed to pause their working relationship might have had nothing to do with honesty. Instead it could have reflected Kavita's commitment to her start-up; the sustainability of her big idea came first. Stepping away from yourself and your own reflexive reactions gives you the chance to operate more mindfully and to reframe your understanding of another stakeholder's actions not as weaknesses and failures but as strengths.

In this chapter, we're going to look at the other side of the "bias" coin: what we frame as biases can just as easily be seen as strengths. This is especially true when working with others. It's easy to see other types of problem solvers as flawed because they aren't like us. But the truth is that the world needs all types of problem solvers because they bring a variety of perspectives to the experience of being human. This reminder was incorporated into the Jewish harvest holiday of Sukkot, when religious Jews shake the lulav and etrog in their sukkahs. The ritual contains four species of plants, lulav, etrog, hadass, and aravah, which are interpreted as representing four different types of people. However, all four species must be brought together to perform the ritual.

I like the symbolism of lulav and etrog because it is a reminder to me of how my Detective "species" is incomplete without the other types. I sometimes struggle when working and making decisions with an Adventurer or a Listener, but the lulav and etrog remind me that we are stronger and make better decisions together and that I can learn from these other PSPs.

While it may be difficult for a Listener to communicate with an Adventurer, we would not want a world of all Listeners—or of all Adventurers. We need rule followers and rule breakers, deep thinkers and committed researchers. That's how we, individually and in community, expand and grow.

Using the language of strength, let's revisit the four most common relationships we all find ourselves in and how to lean into the *strengths* of the different Problem Solver Profiles so that the actions we each take can result in stronger, better decisions with a more likely chance of success. To do that we need to be received positively by our decision-making partners. Although your particular situation might not exactly match any one of the four scenarios below, you can use the scenarios to help you figure out how you might better work with your PSP strengths in combinations with the strengths of those with whom you are working.

Let's see how Saadia, Calvin, Avonelle, and Clara capitalized on their decision-making strengths and used perspective-taking to collaborate more effectively in their decision-making with others. Remember: you're not collaborating just for the sake of collaborating. You're doing it because a decision made in true collaboration has a better chance of succeeding.

Four Scenarios: PSPs and Strengths in Action

Peer to Peer

Saadia and Kavita
Detective/Visionary

The Detective to Visionary decision-making pairing can be a tricky combination because a detail-oriented person is working with someone who is literally the opposite of detailed. It can feel anxiety provoking for the Detective and stifling for the Visionary. But it need not be.

When Saadia, the Detective, felt that her working relationship with Kavita, the Visionary, had been "fractured," she initially wanted to walk away. She decided instead to learn more about what their PSP pairing meant for each of them and their decision-making success. After reading over the Visionary PSP description, strengths and biases (see Cheetah Sheet 6) Saadia reflected that although Kavita had been unable to fulfill her part of the contract, nothing had been decided yet about going forward (or not) with the partnership. Kavita had said she wanted to resume their work together and was continuing to advertise Saadia's blog. What Saadia saw as a "fracture," she realized, might have looked to Visionary Kavita like a bump in the road.

Saadia recognized that her Detective reliance on details and facts had crowded out her attention to anything else, which was a weakness. But she also recognized that as a detail-oriented Detective, she had much to offer a Visionary.

If Saadia hadn't taken the time to assess Kavita's PSP, she might have drawn the conclusion that Kavita was disorganized, or sloppy in her decision-making. By identifying her as a Visionary, Saadia was able to check and challenge her own biases to look at Kavita's strong points to see her as trying to be innovative.

With a new understanding of the relative strengths of their different PSP decision-making approaches, Saadia realized that she had an opportunity to match her own Detective pragmatism with the Visionary's openness to new ideas. She thought about what would work for her and her company, and considered whether, perhaps, she'd want to participate in Kavita's new business in a different way. Given that Visionaries are creative, Saadia came up with a few ideas for alternative compensation plans. One was for some additional in-kind barter agreement that would give Saadia's company access to detailed customer information from Kavita's subscribers and one that would give Saadia options or equity in the future success of Kavita's business. If Saadia could not connect with Kavita's bigger vision, she decided that she should just move on. But if Saadia could speak Kavita's Visionary "language" in a way that worked for both of them, Saadia felt she could create more of a win-win situation.

Hierarchy–Subordinate

Calvin and Talia
Listener/Thinker

Listener to a Thinker: While this pairing works well if the two PSPs are equals working together, in a hierarchical situation, the working style and types of information they value differ and can create conflicts. The Listener wants information from other people and wants connections. The Thinker wants data and its interpretation. Both parties can end up feeling frustrated and unheard.

Calvin, a Listener, was disappointed that his year-end review process seemed to irk his boss Talia, whom he'd pegged as a Thinker. He studied up on the PSP strengths and noticed that a Thinker strength is identifying both pros and cons and being thoughtful. This jibed well with Calvin's listening skills and his desire to grow from Talia's feedback that he should be clearer about what he actually contributed to the teams he works with. He noted that a Listener strength is building a supportive network and being trusting. He decided to lean into those aspects of his PSP to ask Talia for more information up front when she next assigned him to a project. That way, he could better understand what she wanted him to do, which would in turn guide his reporting to her. He also decided to ask some of the other people who work for Talia for tips on working well with her. Calvin now has a plan to come across as the team player he always wanted to be, and that in turn improved his confidence and his own prospects.

Group Dynamic

Avonelle, Dad, and Brother
Detective/Adventurer/Thinker

Detective to Adventurer: Adventurers want to speed up and Detectives like to take their time to gather evidence. Detectives can benefit from Adventurer tendencies by probing the Adventurer about their preferred solution. Detectives can end up feeling left behind or ignored and Adventurers can feel shackled down.

Detective to Thinker: The Detective is proud of and excited by getting "the solution." The Thinker wants to be part of the process of coming to that solution. The Detective can end up thinking her work is unappreciated while the Thinker feels left out and condescended to.

After the holidays, and her frustrating attempt to achieve family unity around COVID restrictions, Detective Avonelle finds herself in the middle of another big family decision. Her Adventurer dad has decided to downsize from his ramshackle five-bedroom house where Avonelle and her brother grew up to a small, two-bedroom condo in a planned senior community. How does Dad decide what to keep, what to give away to family, what to donate, and what to put in the trash? Adventurer Dad just wants it done and is ready to throw everything out, because he wants to focus on the exciting move and the future. Her Thinker brother has a totally different orientation. He wants to have a conversation about almost every single memento in the house and carefully sort the items so that they can be organized into sell, save, give, and toss piles.

Avonelle knows from the COVID situation that she can't make the decisions for her Adventurer dad. He won't view that as helpful, and she'll need to slow down to give her Thinker brother time to process. But she needs Dad to buy into the process too: it's his stuff, and the siblings need his input.

Looking at her and her family members' PSP strengths, Avonelle recognizes that she would have made the downsizing decision very differently, but that Dad's adventurousness is a real strength, and she needs to celebrate that first. So she lets Dad know that she shares his excitement about this big move (even though she'll really miss the family home). Just as she started by speaking to Dad's strength, Avonelle recognizes that she needs to connect with her brother through his strengths too. As a Thinker, he's careful and deliberate, which is why discarding family items is difficult for him. Avonelle knows that as a Detective, she's good at creating an evidence-based plan for how to decide what to keep and what to discard. She also knows that she needs family participation in order for this to succeed, and to create family harmony. So Avonelle essentially creates a rubric by asking her Thinker brother and Adventurer dad to weigh in on the criteria for what to keep and what to discard. By working together to create clear and specific criteria, they all can enjoy keepsakes and feel good about the process.

Hierarchy–Leadership

Clara and Sam
Listener/Visionary

The Visionary is great at dreaming big, and the Listener is good at teasing out insights to help color in the dream's details. But the Listener's questioning to tease out the details can be a buzzkill; they can feel overwhelming and disconnected to the Visionary. From the Listener's point of view, her search for connection can mean that she doesn't communicate clearly.

This can leave her feeling taken advantage of, especially by a Visionary whose main connection is to their ideas.

Visionary Sam has chosen to limit meeting times with his instructional coach, Clara, a Listener, to fifty minutes out of the one-hour slot. Now Clara faces a decision about how much content can realistically be covered in their new shorter sessions. She realizes that she, as the curricular expert, has been determining what they cover. She had never asked him what he found most useful. By examining her own biases and weaknesses, Clara recognized that she was the only one who felt "penalized" by the shorter sessions.

Clara decided that she can use her Listener skills to future-cast with Sam, which allowed him to clarify his Vision of Success. By drawing out Sam's ideal for how he'd like to be remembered by the principal, the students, and his colleagues at year-end, Clara is able to more effectively connect their time together with Sam's goals. She narrowed the details and scope of work to go deep into those issues that build the narrative Sam wants to achieve.

In many situations, when making a decision with others, it's ideal to develop a Vision of Success *with* the other stakeholders in the decision. But there are many instances where that's not going to be comfortable and may not even be possible. When you cannot easily cocreate a Vision of Success, you—like Saadia, Calvin, Avonelle, and Clara—can use Cheetah Sheet 2: Identifying and Understanding Others' PSPs, to assist you in identifying the PSPs of other stakeholders. You may then use the chart in Cheetah Sheet 6: PSP Strengths + Blind Spots, which will assist you in filling out Cheetah Sheet 7: Limiting Biases and the below Cheetah Sheet, which combines your work to check and challenge your biases with bolstering your PSP strengths.

CHEETAH SHEET 9
PSP Strategies to Bolster Strengths and Limit Biases

This Cheetah Sheet is a continuation of Cheetah Sheet 7: Limiting Biases. The first four questions are the same as Cheetah Sheet 7. Begin by bringing those answers down. You will still want to look back at the table in Cheetah Sheet 6: PSPs Strengths + Blind Spots to identify the specific motivations, strengths, and biases that are at work for you and for the other stakeholders in this decision.

1. List your PSP strengths at work in this decision you are faced with.
2. Reframe each of your strengths as potential pitfalls, weakness, or bias. For example, if you pride yourself on your rationality, you may come across to others as cold and distgnt.
3. Think: how might those weaknesses be coming across to the other stakeholders? If you, thinking you're being rational, appear cold and distant, other stakeholders will be afraid to express their feelings because you are not expressing yours.
4. For your other stakeholders, what are you seeing as their weaknesses and biases? Use Cheetah Sheet 6 to review Strengths + Blind Spots.
5. Identify your motivation in the decision. What is driving your need to take action or make a decision?
6. What do you think is motivating other stakeholders? Acknowledge that you're about to make a set of assumptions.
7. How do your strengths work with the other stakeholders' strengths?
8. Where might you come into conflict?
9. Based on your above answers, what are three action steps that would have a good chance of being acceptable to you and well received by the other stakeholder(s)?

Below is instructional coach Clara's exercise for her work with Sam, the young teacher.

COMPLETED CHEETAH SHEET 9
PSP Strategies to Bolster Strengths and Limit Biases. Clara's Example

Clara, an instructional coach, who is a Listener, is working with Sam, a young teacher. Clara felt that her work with Sam wasn't as effective as it could be and was frustrated by this. She used Cheetah Sheet 3: Identifying and Understanding Others' PSPs to identify Sam as a Visionary. She checked her biases with Cheetah Sheet 7: Limiting Biases. She now uses this Cheetah Sheet to future-cast the way her decision will play out.

1. List your PSP strengths at work in this decision you are faced with.
   I see myself as relational, trusting, and supportive.
2. Reframe each of your strengths as potential pitfalls, weakness, or bias. For example, if you pride yourself on your rationality, you may come across to others as cold and distant.
   a. **I realize that my desire for connection means that I work to avoid any whiff of conflict.**
   b. **I realize that what I see as trusting is an assumption that Sam values the same things I do. His values may not be mine.**
   c. **I realize that what I see as supportiveness can come across as controlling to others. I want to meet for an hour because, as a Listener, I value in-person contact. I realized that other PSPs might feel supported (and be supportive) without needing so much in-person time.**
3. Think: how might those weaknesses be coming across to the other stakeholders?
   a. **I realize that because I prioritize being relational and connected I may have successfully hidden from Sam my perception that there is a problem with Sam's lateness.**
   b. **I realize that I trust Sam to prioritize what I value but I haven't discussed those values, which in this instance means being on time. I haven't asked Sam what he values; perhaps he values our time together so much that he needs a few minutes to switch from his teacher head to being a student himself.**
   c. **I realize I have no idea what Sam considers to be supportive. Perhaps he feels very supported by the time and content that we explore together.**
4. For your other stakeholders, what are you seeing as their weaknesses and biases? Again use Cheetah Sheet 6 to review Strengths + Blind Spots.
   I see Sam as flighty, unreliable, and disorganized.
5. Identify your motivation in the decision. What is driving your need to take action or make a decision?
   I'm motivated by feeling frustrated and angry that Sam is late, which makes me feel disrespected by him. Having completed Cheetah Sheet 7, and looking at my biases and Sam's strengths, I realize that I haven't been

clear to Sam about my feelings. I also realize I was framing the problem as that he was losing out on important instructional time, but actually we'd been functioning in the shorter time period and Sam had been taking those lessons to heart and benefiting from our work.

6. What do you think is motivating other stakeholders? Acknowledge that you're about to make a set of assumptions.
   I think Sam is motivated to be a good teacher. He wants to do right by his students. I realize that I was so focused on feeling disrespected that I lost sight of the fact that Sam values being the best teacher he can be.

7. How do your strengths work with the other stakeholders' strengths?
   As a Listener, I want to help Sam and give him the benefit of my experience. As a Visionary, I believe that Sam wants to learn from me. I realize that we are aligned in our strengths.

8. Where might you come into conflict?
   The only problem, I now realize, is the small time problem.

9. Based on your above answers, what are three action steps that would have a good chance of being acceptable to you and *well received by the other stakeholder(s)*?
   I will put my path forward into action by:
   - Future-casting with Sam about his success at year-end from the vantage points of the principal, students, and colleagues. This will get to Sam's strength as a creative thinker and give us a path forward.
   - The future-casting can then lead us to identifying concrete objectives to measure success from each perspective.
   - Using these concrete objectives we can lay out a pathway for future sessions so that I can help him travel from where he is now to achieving the success that he wants—and that I want for him and for myself as an instructional coach.

It's easy—particularly for people we know well—to say, "she's always late" or "it's because he is a creative person," but don't let your preconceived notions about yourself and others determine the PSP you apply to the other person. Look past your biases to actual behavior. That was my mistake with my mom—I saw her as "Dr. Mom," a Thinker, because she is a Thinker in professional situations. But when I looked at her behavior with her family, I realized that she was an Adventurer.

Chapter Thirteen

How PSPs Color Our Relationship with Data

As far as the laws of mathematics refer to reality, they are not certain,
and as far as they are certain, they do not refer to reality.
–Albert Einstein

As Ari and Tim settled on their path forward to stop sex trafficking in India by interrupting criminal networks, they wanted a metric to communicate to potential funders Protect Her Life's expected impact. They knew that the Pareto Principle applied in all kinds of diverse situations: 20 percent of drivers cause 80 percent of accidents; 20 percent of polluters are responsible for 80 percent of pollution; and, a little closer to their hearts, 20 percent of criminals are responsible for 80 percent of crimes. They'd been thinking that the 80/20 rule must therefore apply to sex trafficking: 80 percent of the girls entering the trafficking system were coming from just 20 percent of the criminal networks. By extrapolation, they had become convinced that their organization could reduce sex trafficking by 80 percent within two years (and were preparing donor material making the claim)—provided that they identified and disrupted that key 20 percent of criminal networks.

They believed that the outcome could be verified by a third party. They imagined that baseline and end-line studies could be done to collect data on how many girls under eighteen were being forced into sex work at the baseline and how many were being forced two years later. They were fixated on the wow factor of an 80 percent decrease. It was a salient number that, they believed, would impress their funders.

But where was the data? Could they make such a claim without evidence? Could they assume that the Pareto Principle even applied to sex trafficking in India? Even if the data about sex trafficking were available, how could they be sure of Protect Her Life's impact? What outcomes were actually being measured by Protect Her Life's day-to-day work—or the proposed two-year study?

I pointed out that while a before-and-after measure by a third party *would* give some information about how many girls the study could count, the data itself wouldn't necessarily provide any information about Protect Her Life's impact. It would be a point-in-time study, and it would only cover some number of locations. Whatever numbers it did report *could* show some correlation to Protect Her Life's activities, but they wouldn't provide any information about causation. The point-in-time study also wouldn't let Ari and Tim know which of Protect Her Life's activities were successful and which ones were not.

I suggested that if Ari and Protect Her Life still wanted to use the 80 percent figure, they needed to use it differently: to frame the problem, not the organization's impact. Maybe Protect Her Life could instead explain to their funders how a small number of criminal networks have an outsized impact on trafficking, and how that data would inform their organization's mission and strategy. But they couldn't make claims about their efficacy without data—which did not (yet) exist.

This conversation opened Ari's eyes to the fact that the Problem Solver Profile strengths and biases don't just play out in how we engage with people; they also interfere with how we locate, identify, understand, and use data. Ari's Visionary lens led him to glom onto the Pareto Principle's 80–20 theory, map it onto criminal activity related to sex trafficking, and then use it in a way that reflected his bold and optimistic outlook on what Protect Her Life could accomplish. He didn't see that while the crime data might be salient, it didn't necessarily automatically apply to all criminal networks—or to the criminal networks in the region where his organization was operating. What looked to be true globally may not be true locally.

What's more, because Protect Her Life was engaging in so many different activities, including locating and mapping the criminal networks, the locations where sex trafficking was occurring, and the girls and women in the system, the organization had no idea which of these activities actually had an impact. Did they really need all this mapping and intelligence? Was some of it more relevant—and useful—to their efforts? Collecting that kind of data would be informative, but where was the wow for funders?

Ari was so focused on the wow that he didn't recognize that funders might want less sexy but more relevant data.

PSP Data Preferences

Each PSP has a unique lens on the world, and this lens colors how decision makers gather, understand, and organize incoming information. At times, data collection works well, but at times our predilections trip us up. Being aware of how you as a problem solver prefer to engage with data is a necessary precursor to using data more effectively. It's not something that we tend to think about, but it is a topic that was very much on my mind when I began working with people who wanted to learn and apply the AREA Method.

I had developed the AREA Method when I was an investigative journalist, concerned with feeling confident that I was conducting sound research. I wanted a way to check and challenge how I gathered and analyzed evidence to ensure that I didn't fall for the bait of my inner voice's potentially false judgments.

I constructed AREA as a perspective-taking system that would guide users to separate out and categorize information according to the source of that information. AREA delineates between primary and secondary sources, and between document-based sources and data collected via conversations and interviews. This approach to data collection allows stakeholders to become aware of assumptions and judgments. By separating information sources into four categories, each representing a different point of view, users can more easily understand each one and identify disagreements or disparities between them. The organized approach assesses all the angles of a story and highlights how the findings may be interpreted by the various stakeholders.

However, as a Detective—and a trained journalist—I assumed that my desire to gather all kinds of data and to check and challenge my biases was shared by everyone. But when AREA went out into the world, people applied the system as *they* are—not as *I am*.

A system like AREA *does* work, but I began to see that users needed to first do the spadework to understand how they approach their decision-making to face their own biases so that they could deliberately work against those biases.

An example: In my first book, *Problem Solved*, I chronicled the story of an amazing young man named John Christopher, who had started a basic health care charity called the Oda Foundation in rural Nepal. When we met, John was thinking about expanding his charity's health care offerings, but the very evening that we spoke, a devastating earthquake hit Nepal, killing over ten thousand people. Overnight, John's long-term desire to expand became a problem that needed to be addressed immediately. But how?

He'd been predisposed to opening a second health care clinic in a more populous area; his first clinic had been a great success. As a Thinker and secondarily as a Listener—which I didn't recognize at the time—John was someone who not only weighed available options in relation to one another, comparing them within a context, but also prioritized his human connections, relying on input from trusted friends and mentors for his big decisions. So for John, data felt limiting and just wasn't as important as face-to-face, qualitative information-gathering through the relationships he'd developed.

John trusted his observations and his own personal experience, sometimes at the expense of data. Further, he assumed, because whatever data he might locate would be coming from the government of Nepal, an emerging nation, whatever might exist would be stale, out of date, or incomplete. In other words, without looking for, or at, the data, John decided it wouldn't be useful.

Because we were collaborating on John's problem-solving, I led him to the realization that there was too much at stake to make the decision without at least seeing what data was out there. It turned out that John found usable data—and data that he could put to the test as he made his big decision. John had framed the problem too narrowly, assuming that only data from the Nepalese government would be useful. But he discovered that there were a host of other experienced charities out there that provided basic health care in emerging nations—and that these organizations had gathered their own data about Nepal and its health care needs. They had their own insights on health care delivery in the very area where John was working.

John had another blind spot. In considering options besides a second clinic, John ruled out partnering with the Nepalese government to provide services because he'd heard of several instances in which the government clinics provided poor health care. John extrapolated this pattern of data as a system-wide problem and allowed it to shut down his thinking in this area.

These two instances show that his assumptions about data—incorrectly framing the problem of data sources and mistaking multiple data points for a persistent and pervasive pattern—almost bankrupted the Oda Foundation. When John looked beyond the narrow frame he was operating in, he did find population data for the busier location where he was considering a second clinic. The numbers were much larger than he anticipated, and more than one new clinic could handle. John realized that Oda didn't have the resources to serve so many people.

At the same time, AREA's perspective-taking, looking at the problem from a variety of stakeholder lenses to understand their thoughts, incentives, and motives, led John to a new and broader understanding of what "basic health care" meant. This led him to think about other services Oda could provide. Further, he came to see that local leaders living near government clinics could serve as emissaries and influencers to vouch for Oda's independence from the government and for its track record of providing quality care. Partnering with the government didn't have to mean that Oda's reputation would suffer.

At the time of John's decision, it made sense for him to fall back onto personal experience and the charity's current success with its original clinic. It also made sense to rely on the information John had learned from locals with their experience at government clinics. Like John, we are all constantly collecting information, thinking that the information tells a story, and we often think, therefore, that we already have all the information we need.

John made what appeared to be sensible assumptions, but he did them from a Thinker and Listener's perspective. My Detective approach led John to a more thorough decision-making process.

Data Traps

How do you check and challenge your decision tendencies without me riding sidecar?

That's what led to the development of the Problem Solver Profiles—to allow each of you to see your biases and blind spots when I'm not there to point them out. However, data is tricky, and all of the Problem

Solver Profiles can be tripped up by data in different ways. Particularly when you're rushing to make a decision, you tend to fall back on decision-making patterns that are comfortable and that may have worked in the past—or even may not have. So how do you confront what you think you "know"?

How do you move forward with a decision when you don't have expertise—whether you're deciding which washing machine to buy, where to have your baby, or which college or university to attend? And when do you challenge your own expertise so that you expand your thinking? Often, the data out there seems actionable but shouldn't be.

Identify the Category of Data with Which You Are Working

There are three main kinds of data we often confront and feel compelled to act on: **salient data,** like Ari's reliance on the Pareto Principle, which captures our attention because it is noteworthy or surprising; **contextual data,** which has a frame that may impact how we interpret it; and **patterned data,** like John's assumption about the unreliability of government data, which appears to have a regular, intelligible, and meaningful form.

- **Salient data** can activate *salience bias*, in which we overweight new or noteworthy information, resulting in suboptimal decision-making, planning errors, and more. For example, airline passenger demand in April 2020 plunged over 94 percent compared with April 2019, because of COVID-related travel restrictions. That shocking statistic might make us think that travel as we have come to know it is finished—but in reality, this one salient piece of data tells us almost nothing about future travel.
- **Contextual data** can constrict our thinking and lead to a *framing bias:* the context in which we receive the data impacts how we think about it. For example, "80 percent lean ground beef" sounds more healthful than "beef with 20 percent fat." But it's the same beef, framed differently.
- **Patterned data** often prompts the *clustering illusion*—also known in sports and gambling as the "hot hand fallacy"— whereby we assume that random events are information that

will help us predict a future event. The human brain is wired to look for patterns, sometimes when they don't exist. Equally important, when patterns do exist, they often don't have predictive value. A die that turns up a two several times in a row has established a pattern, but that says nothing about what the next roll will be.

How PSPs Interact with Data

Different PSPs tend to favor different kinds of data. Salient data tends to be attractive to Visionaries who are thinking big—like Ari. Contextual data often speaks to the Thinkers who want to frame a problem. Patterned data is comfortable for Detectives, looking to corroborate what they think they already know and being led by data that fits their worldview. Listeners looking for a handle on how to think about a problem tend to collect qualitative data, opinions relating to the situations they find themselves in. And while data might have a place for Adventurers, data itself is not the most important factor in making decisions, and so they may be more naturally skeptical and therefore less likely to be heavily influenced by different kinds of data.

Below is a Cheetah Sheet of the most common data analysis traps for each of the PSPs. It also contains a question that the PSP can ask of him/herself when dealing with data and a question for the stakeholder working with that PSP. I also encourage you to make yourself familiar with the three most common kinds of data that can fool us, especially if we're not used to or not comfortable with interpreting data, or making a decision in an area where we don't feel we have expertise.

CHEETAH SHEET 10
PSP Data Traps

Use this chart to familiarize yourself with the most common data analysis traps for each of the PSPs. Use the two Question columns to counter data traps associated with each PSP.

PSP	Relationship to Data	Data Trap	Questions for the PSP	Questions if you are working with a specific PSP
Adventurer	Suspicious of data and even oppositional to it.	Relies on instinct and wants to move forward.	Adventurer: Remind yourself that not everyone likes to make decisions on instinct.	Is there some data that can inform your decision that you haven't already gathered? Have you looked for disconfirming data to check your present path?
Detective	May over-rely on data.	Patterned data: Seeing a pattern even where there isn't one.	Detective: Can you establish the criteria for data collection before you begin your decision-making to minimize the likelihood of seeing a pattern that may not exist and prevent you from cherry-picking among facts?	Can you establish ahead of time how much data will be collected and criteria for collection and evaluation?

PSP	Relationship to Data	Data Trap	Questions for the PSP	Questions if you are working with a specific PSP
Listener	Rely on qualitative data collected through personal interactions.	Suspicious of data without a personal connection.	Listener: Make sure you begin your data collection by sharing with your trusted sources your Vision of Success and goals for your decision.	Can you make sure that the Listener has done more than listen and that she has contributed her thoughts? Have you asked the Listener to share her values around data?
Thinker	May rely on data to solve a problem, but they privilege their own thinking process.	They can miss the problem for the process, incorrectly framing the problem and its context.	Thinker: Write down the problem you are solving for and your Vision of Success to prevent the process from taking over the problem.	Can you develop together a Vision of Success and use this as the touchstone to keep Thinkers on track to guide the decision process?
Visionary	May look for a piece of, or a limited amount of, exciting information.	May incorrectly assign significance to eye-catching or salient data.	Visionary: Real-time feedback can help you adapt and make better decisions. Get feedback from the people around you before acting alone on the data.	Ask for other data to support the decision. Can you help Visionaries step back to see the bigger picture and put salient data into context?

Recognizing how each of these categories triggers our biases can prevent us from falling prey to those biases, but how do we move forward once we've accepted that we need additional information or insight to confidently make decisions about the future?

Come Back to Inversion

How can you improve how you work with information? Here's where you come back to inversion, using your goal, to craft a Vision of Success: *What matters to you in the outcome of the decision?* There will likely be an endless amount of data that could be acquired to help you make your decision (and if you're a Detective you might just try to get it all), but that's not useful. By inverting the problem, you can narrow down the types and amount of data you need. Inversion will help you home in on those you deem to be critical to solving your specific problem with confidence.

In Ari's case, for example, when he inverted the problem of what data to use to hold his organization accountable for their work, he realized he didn't really need to know the number of girls trafficked to be successful because his organization wasn't focused on that; it was focused on the criminal activity that perpetuated trafficking. The Vision of Success was to disrupt the traffickers so *they* couldn't continue trafficking girls.

This realization made it easier for Ari to step back from his excitement about applying the salient Pareto Principle to his charity's impact. In the absence of data, Ari couldn't assume that the Pareto Principle was relevant for sex traffickers in India, and a point-in-time measurement of the girls and women who were working as sex workers (which was flawed data to begin with) wouldn't tell Ari anything about his organization's impact on the criminal networks that were trafficking these women.

By refocusing on his organization's Vision of Success, Ari could now see his bigger picture more clearly. His organization did not know how to stop 80 percent of girls being trafficked. But it could identify and interrupt the most active criminal networks involved in trafficking, whether they were responsible for 80 percent or 40 percent of the women being trafficked. It helped him better understand Protect Her Life's mission and focus on realistic impact—that his organization could make an impact, but in the short term, he couldn't claim ready to assign some dramatic percentage reduction to the terrible problem Protect Her Life was tackling overall. That sex trafficking would continue to be a problem was, sadly, a "known known."

There were still so many unknowns. But now with the Vision of Success, the range of "known unknowns" became easier to deal with. Ari and Protect Her Life realized that yes, they could solve their data-specific problem without solving for all the trafficking unknowns because they only had to solve for the data that mattered to how Protect Her Life carried out its mission.

Formulate the Right Questions to Get the Answers You Need

Many of us have trouble crafting the questions that could help us make a decision. For Ari and Protect Her Life, I suggested looking at the problem from a variety of perspectives to better understand how the issue might be viewed from other vantage points. For Ari and for you, a practical way to think about the questions to ask is to organize them into four main categories: behavior, opinion, feeling, and knowledge. These four lenses together form a 360-degree look at the kinds of information that can be knowable. We can glean data about what someone does, what they experience emotionally, what they think, and what they can substantiate.

By asking questions that get at these different categories of what is knowable, Ari ensured that his organization would bring distance and a variety of responses to the way they probed their data, which would help counter preconceived assumptions and judgments. It would also give them a better context for interpreting the answers, because they could know the lens through which the questions were being filtered.

Below is a Cheetah Sheet for Great Questions broken down into the four perspectives of questions. Readers of *Problem Solved* and *Investing in Financial Research* may recall them from AREA Exploration. Following the general questions are the questions Ari and Protect Her Life asked themselves as they moved forward in their decision-making process.

CHEETAH SHEET 11
Types of Great Questions

Use this glossary when you need to gather information to craft great questions. Applying wording related to the specific information perspective you want to learn about will elicit practical and actionable answers.

- Behavior questions address what someone does or has done. They will yield descriptions of actual experiences, activities, and actions. Ari asked: Which criminal activity is the most central to interrupting human trafficking? How do the networks bring the girls into the system, and how do they force them into becoming sex workers?

- Opinion questions tackle what someone thinks about a topic, action, or event. They can get at people's goals, intentions, desires, and values. Ari asked: What's the best-case scenario if we intervene at the touchpoints that we've identified? What's the worst-case scenario if we intervene at the identified touchpoints? If we can remove criminals from the network, how easy/hard will it be for them to be replaced? What is the most effective way we can partner with other organizations to increase the impact of the work?

- Feeling questions ask how someone responds emotionally to a topic. They can help you get beyond factual information to learn what people may be inclined to do regardless of the data. Ari asked: How does my team feel about where to interrupt criminal activity for the most systemic impact? Do we feel this data will feel meaningful to funders?

- Knowledge questions explore what factual information the respondent has about your topic. While some may argue that all knowledge is a set of beliefs, knowledge questions assess what the person being questioned considers to be factual. Ari asked: What can past criminal arrests tell us about changes in trafficking activity? Has criminal network activity been studied? Who else might have data?

Using this approach led Ari and Protect Her Life to several realizations. First, by asking the behavior questions, they realized that although they had data about which criminals were linked to direct brothel activities, they didn't know much about the start of the pipeline. Second, by asking his team their opinion, Ari was able to understand their thinking about the most positive and negative implications of their options. Third, the feeling questions led them to explore whether it would feel satisfying for the organization to take on criminal networks instead of conducting dramatic rescues. Asking these questions led Ari to realize that, although the work of disrupting the trafficking system had the potential to be far more impactful in the long run, the emotional high of freeing any number of girls was important to him and to Protect Her Life. Ari knew they needed to shift the organization's resources to a replicable and financially sustainable methodology that would allow them to primarily focus on systemic outcomes. He also recognized that they needed to find a way to continue the emotionally satisfying work of rescuing girls. Fourth and finally, the knowledge questions led them to realize that they needed to gather more data to find evidence about criminal trafficking arrests linked to brothels.

Ari realized that they didn't have data about the beginning of the trafficking process, but they did have data about the different locations where sex work was occurring and how those locations were tied to criminal networks. He also realized that there were some criminals who were working in more than one location. They hypothesized that removing those "super-spreaders" could cause systemic damage. What remained unknown was whether weakening that link would actually cause systemic damage. Would activities cease at a location, or would the network be easily able to replace that person? Could removing one person at a nexus sow distrust between different networks, and therefore have a multiplier effect to weaken sex trafficking?

By inverting his problem-solving, Ari was able to focus on the known unknowns that mattered to their specific activities. Now the charity knew what they wanted to count, why they were counting those things, and what to look for in the data to know whether their work was succeeding and to make future decisions about the organization's path.

You can ask these types of questions about any kind of incomplete data: salient, contextual, and/or patterned. The four perspectives of questions acknowledge that uncertainty is a mix of actions and reactions, opinion, knowledge, and emotion. Classifying and addressing the ingredients in the uncertainty mixture won't gain us certainty, but we can be sure that our questions speak to all areas of uncertainty to better manage the role of emotion and bias in our decision-making, to name and confront our reactions to information, and to move forward with a more rational and carefully made decision. Taking the time to ask these types of questions can also provide clarity, both individually and for an organization. Having a record of how a particular decision was made provides transparency and an audit trail that prevents evolving hypotheses and allows an assessment for better future decisions.

The Great Questions road map can improve your ability to get practical and actionable information, but since conversation is a two-way radio, you can also use the road map to better listen to others and understand what kind of information they are asking for. The next Cheetah Sheet provides you with a brief quiz to improve your understanding of someone else's question cues and signals so that your responses may be more accurate, complete, and useful.

Voltaire once famously recommended that we judge a man by his questions rather than his answers. We'll never know the future, but by honing our ability to formulate and respond to questions tailored to elicit specific kinds of information, we can better examine our data, our thinking, and the informational needs of others.

CHEETAH SHEET 12
Types of Great Questions Quiz

Use this quiz to ensure you understand the different types of great questions. In the future, use this quiz to check that you're crafting questions to elicit the kind of information you want to glean.

Bringing distance and a variety of perspectives to the way you probe your data can counter preconceived assumptions and judgments. They can also provide you with a better context for interpreting the answers because you'll be making explicit the different lenses through which answers are filtered. The first time through, ensure you understand the different types of questions. In the future, use this quiz to check that you've included interview questions that get at all four of the types of Great Questions.

1. Question starters:
   • What data or information do you have about . . . ?
   • What evidence supports your thinking about . . . ?
2. Question starters:
   • What do you think about . . . ?
   • What's your opinion on . . . ?

3. Question starters:
   - What actions . . . ?
   - How do you behave when . . . ?
4. Question starters:
   - How do you feel about . . . ?
   - What emotions were present when . . . ?

Answer Key:

1 = Knowledge questions. Explore what factual information the respondent has about your topic. While some may argue that all knowledge is a set of beliefs, knowledge questions assess what the person being questioned considers to be factual.

2 = Opinion questions. Tackle what someone thinks about a topic, action, or event. They can get at people's goals, intentions, desires, and values.

3 = Behavior questions. Address what someone does or has done and will yield descriptions of actual experiences, activities, and actions.

4 = Feeling questions. Ask how someone responds emotionally to a topic. They can help you get beyond factual information to learn what people may be inclined to do regardless of the data.

The four lenses help you better address your emotional responses, name and confront them, and move forward with a rational decision. They will give you a more complete picture, reducing the likelihood that you'll rely on well-worn thinking pathways and cognitive biases.

Chapter Fourteen

Situationality and Dynamic Decision-Making

The right formula for success is patience in the mind
and dynamism in action.
—Gurudev Sri Sri Ravi Shankar

Get ready to retake the PSP module again.

Now that you've had a chance to think deeply about yourself as a problem solver and to check and challenge your patterns of acting, reacting, and interacting with others around decision-making, it's time to go deeper. The truth is, we all make decisions in different ways depending on the context and the other decision makers we are engaging with. How an established surgeon in her fifties, for example, makes decisions at work may differ greatly from how she makes decisions at home and may also differ from how she made decisions when she was a resident in training. The same is likely true for you too, which is why I'm going to ask you at the end of this chapter to take the PSP quiz again.

What does it look like for someone to have a dominant and secondary PSP? Working with Ari and Tim I saw this in action, and their experience provides a good window into the power of secondary PSPs.

Several months after I began working with Ari, I asked his business partner, Tim, to take the PSP assessment. To no one's surprise, Tim was a Visionary. Having two Visionaries at the helm of a new charity may have partly accelerated Protect Her Life's momentum because they fed each other's big dreams. However, Tim and Ari are much more than just business partners; they had met in college at a party, and they formed such a strong friendship that they became roommates. They maintained their friendship as they both headed out into the work world. When Ari called Tim after that initial trip to India, fired up about ending sex trafficking in India, he asked Tim to quit his job. Tim did. Tim definitely *is* a Visionary like Ari, so he was excited about this grand idea. But his willingness to follow Ari's lead suggested to me that he had another, secondary, PSP.

I asked Tim to retake the PSP quiz, but to focus on his relationship with Ari. The result: Tim's secondary PSP is a Listener. When he realized he had this strong secondary PSP, Tim said, "It made sense to me since I love taking guidance and hearing people's perspectives. I was pretty surprised initially, but then after more thought I realized it made a lot of sense. I realized that I've been embracing my inner Listener."

This new information explained a lot about Tim and Ari's personal and professional relationship. Early on in the creation of the charity, Tim recognized that somebody needed to be the brakes on their grand plans, and he took that job on. However, it was so uncomfortable for him that Tim quickly gave up on it. Learning that he was a Listener who wants to build positive relationships with others, Tim understood where his reluctance was coming from: listeners don't like conflict, and being a naysayer to Ari's grand ideas felt like conflict.

We saw this same dynamic with Clara, the learning specialist, who didn't want to be firm with Sam, the young teacher she was mentoring. She, like many Listeners, wanted to come to agreement. Amity is very important to the Listener.

But for Tim, dealing with a gung-ho Visionary, amity was hard to achieve when it meant getting Ari to agree to scale back his grand plans. Being the brakes "wasn't my natural state," Tim noted. He felt more comfortable and happier when he could be the cheerleader; it was harder to be the voice of reason (and less fun).

Through our work, learning about the Listener's strengths gave Tim validation that, although it did not feel natural to be the "crossing guard" for Ari's ideas, his discomfort and negative feelings around acting as a Listener did not mean it was the wrong thing for him to be doing. *Hard* was not the same as *bad*. Tim came to see that his Listener skills were an important balance to Ari's Visionary ideas. Further, he realized he could use the PSP Listener template to lean in to skills he wanted to develop. "I began to put on that hat for the good of the organization. I came to see Ari as the Visionary and to see myself and my role as helping to guide ideas and make them actionable. I don't just provide brakes. I provide color and context; I look at the pros and cons and the data to turn ideas into reality or shoot them down."

Like Tim, you are not only one kind of decision maker, even though you may have identified a dominant approach that you've tended to use in the past. You, like all of us, are a dynamic decision maker. You have other decision approach tendencies at times influenced by both prior experience and by the current situation you find yourself in. Like the muscles we build when we exercise, you can intentionally grow and change as a decision maker to be a "better" version of yourself and one with greater agency in the world, but first you need to know more about yourself and the situations you find yourself in. It's not always comfortable, or easy, but like weight lifters who work on their mobility to become better weight lifters, working on decision-making skills that don't come naturally will make you a better all-around decision maker.

Not all of us will fit Tim's profile of having a weak, but necessary, secondary PSP. Sometimes your secondary PSP can overwhelm or subvert your primary profile. Miriam, for example, is the chief executive and founder of an agriculture technology start-up company. She identified herself as a Listener. She told me, "I enjoy listening to the perspectives of others on any topic because I understand that we all think differently, that most solutions are not black and white. I like understanding the effects of the solution on different types of individuals or groups, which can make one decision more impactful than the other." Like other Listeners, Miriam makes new friends easily and connects with strangers virtually everywhere she goes.

However, shortly after we began working on her company's strategy and growth plans, Miriam confessed that her cofounder, Elon, with whom she had been working remotely, had suddenly stopped communicating. The start-up was in a delicate stage, and Elon was responsible for writing a grant proposal for some much-needed funding. After numerous attempts to reach him, Miriam finally decided that she had to alert Elon that he was in violation of their partnership agreement. Given the company's critical financial state, Miriam, as the majority owner, informed Elon that she would begin a fundraising round without him and would buy out his ownership stake. Typically, this kind of acrimony would be very difficult for anyone, particularly for a Listener, who values relationships and tends to excel at them. I commented on this to Miriam, who confessed that "maintaining relationships is a struggle for me, even with close friends. I've been told by friends that they don't feel like I am there for them."

When I asked her to elaborate, she said, "I care about how I'm seen in a social setting, but I don't necessarily adapt my behavior or opinions if I don't agree with others." Miriam also noted that although she enjoyed hearing others' opinions and ideas, "I prefer to make my own interpretation of a situation rather than taking someone else's for granted."

This apparent contradiction of listening but then dismissing the views of others was unusual for a Listener. Indeed, Miriam admitted, "I want to do better with relationships." Was something perhaps interfering with her first inclination to hear from—and to learn with—others? I asked Miriam to retake the PSP focused on her relationships. The result: Miriam's secondary PSP is the Adventurer.

Miriam immediately understood the implications: "My Adventurer is sabotaging my Listener," she said with new awareness. She agreed that she had all of the Adventurer strengths as well as the blind spots of optimism, planning, and confirmation biases. "I am quite confident when I make decisions and sometimes even a bit too quick to make them, relying on my gut." She also recognized the impact her Adventurer self had on her friendships: she wasn't making time to check in and connect with her friends because "my Adventurer says 'we're friends already,' so why should I have to worry about them?" It was this Adventurer self that led her friends to feel that she wasn't truly there for them. Miriam also came to see that her Adventurer side found developing new friendships more fulfilling than keeping up with old ones.

Through our work, Miriam saw that she'd allowed the narrative bias, often a problem for Listeners, to act as a self-fulling prophecy. She'd taken the comments made by those couple of friends and constructed a story about herself as someone who just wasn't good at relationships. Instead of working on her relationships, she'd decided to focus her energies elsewhere, justifying her decision to walk away from friends because she had a higher calling to develop her nascent technology. She would change people's lives for the better; the loss of a few friends was a necessary price to pay.

I pointed out to Miriam that we all are in relationships, all the time. She might have been perfectly willing to ignore and even disappoint her friends, but her role as the CEO of a start-up meant she was in *work* relationships. And she was going to have to make *those* relationships work if she wanted to see her new technology brought to market. Even more, Miriam herself would ultimately feel happier, and more fulfilled and successful, by nurturing important professional—and personal—relationships.

Both Miriam and Tim saw themselves as stuck in situations that were harmful personally and professionally. They had no control—or so they thought. They thought that they were who they were. Too often that's the message of self-assessments like Myers-Briggs or the Five Factor Personality Test: who we are is "fixed" and predetermined, because we have a set of characteristics that are essentialist, making us who we are—and that we should embrace those confines.

Problem Solver Profiles are not proscriptive. They are dynamic. They are meant to be used not as labels but as guide wires, allowing us to move dynamically within complex relationships and through complicated decision-making situations.

Tim and Miriam were not "fixed." The reality is that they didn't know what to do because they had habits of behavior and decision-making; those habits made them feel stuck. They took that "stuckness" as immobility. But through our work together, they both began to see that there were specific actions they could take that would allow them to be more effective as decision makers, as professionals, and as human beings.

What specific steps did Tim and Miriam take to assess their situations? The good news for you is that the steps they each took are repeatable and can be followed as a rubric. Below you'll find the Dynamic Decision-Making Cheetah Sheet. It explains, side by side, how the Problem Solver Profiles operate and how situationality impacts us in our decision-making and our relationships.

I touched on this briefly in chapter 2 when I outlined that there are three distinct and different benefits to understanding and being familiar with all of the decision-making archetypes: creating a shared lexicon; building effective community; and discerning situationality. Briefly, a shared lexicon gives you a vocabulary and language for exploring the different problem-solving approaches. Building an effective community is about understanding that different decision-making styles are not "better" or "worse," because they all have strengths and weaknesses; recognizing the value of each approach allows us to more easily learn from and with one another to explore decisions from a variety of perspectives, even when they may not be natural for your own PSP. Discerning situationality recognizes that the same decision maker makes decisions differently depending on who we are deciding with and what we are deciding about.

Situationality, however, is not only about the external who and what. *It is also about who you are internally.* You are not static; you are ever changing. Thinking about situationality means looking at yourself as though you are a character in a story: How old are you? Where are you located in both space and time, that is, in your life journey? Who else is in the scene and how central are you to the action? And how important is the action to you?

Using the PSPs and related tools, you can not only identify your situationality but also learn to direct it. You can try on the PSPs for different decisions the way you try new clothes. As you hone your skills, you might decide to take a vacation as an Adventurer, allowing you to free yourself from your daily worries and to make decisions in the moment. Or you might try buying insurance like a Detective because you are actively looking to mitigate risk. Using your situationality, you can examine competing decision impulses to better understand the psychology of decision-making and bolster new decision skills.

Often, in our lives and for many of the decisions we make, we don't need to slow down our decision-making process and take time-consuming steps. However, if like Tim and Miriam you are dissatisfied or stuck, or your decision-making style is creating conflict in situations you care about, or you're facing a consequential decision that you are hesitant to move forward and make, then the metacognition of this process can give you a better path forward.

Below I've recapped these key ideas about Problem Solver Profiles in a graphic organizer. Use this chart as a reference to understand the theory of change behind our personal decision-making habits and patterns and how our ecosystem impacts and changes our plans. By keeping the Dynamic Decision-Making Cheetah Sheet handy, you can better harness your decision dynamism.

CHEETAH SHEET 13
Dynamic Decision-Making

Use this table as a synopsis for the Theory of Change behind Problem Solver Profiles and Dynamic Decision-Making.

PSP CONCEPT	PSP SITUATIONALITY
Concept: What is a Problem Solver Profile? PSPs describe five different common approaches to decision-making and their related strengths and weaknesses.	
Different people have different kinds of decision-making approaches.	Decision-making styles are contextual, not rigid, and they vary depending on four factors: place, life stage, people, and decision ownership.
How each concept plays out: Different PSPs prioritize different kinds of input and information and therefore solve problems optimizing for different things.	
Your PSP is a muscle: as you use it, you strengthen it and get better at it. But you may be ignoring other muscles. For example: the more gratified you are by using the data, the more you feel validated that your Detective data-driven decision-making approach is the best way to go.	Context: We make decisions differently based on what's going on around us, who we are with, how old we are, how much expertise we have, how much we care about the decision, and how we feel physically and emotionally.
Behavioral patterns: Because the PSPs optimize for different kinds of solutions, they tend to behave differently when solving problems.	
Curse of experience: The more your decision-making style works for you, the more convinced you are that it is the only style.	Situational blindness: We often don't see the fullness of the situation we are in, and we don't recognize how it's influencing our decision-making abilities.
How can you grow as a problem solver? PSPs are not proscriptive. By increasing your awareness of the different decision-making approaches and situationality, you can adopt new decision skills and strengthen your relationships with others.	
The PSP is not prescriptive or absolute. It reflects what you've tended to do in the past, in a given situation. It's a mirror that shows you how you see yourself in the world; it shows you what you think is dominant about how you make decisions. Knowing what you're looking at allows you to confront—and challenge—that self-perception.	Use the Secondary PSP Cheetah Sheet: By retaking the PSP and understanding your secondary PSP you can figure out what other decision-making patterns you employ. You can assess whether your secondary PSP helps your dominant PSP or undercuts it.

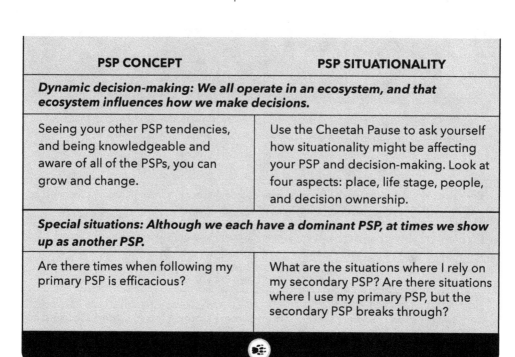

PSP CONCEPT	PSP SITUATIONALITY
Dynamic decision-making: We all operate in an ecosystem, and that ecosystem influences how we make decisions.	
Seeing your other PSP tendencies, and being knowledgeable and aware of all of the PSPs, you can grow and change.	Use the Cheetah Pause to ask yourself how situationality might be affecting your PSP and decision-making. Look at four aspects: place, life stage, people, and decision ownership.
Special situations: Although we each have a dominant PSP, at times we show up as another PSP.	
Are there times when following my primary PSP is efficacious?	What are the situations where I rely on my secondary PSP? Are there situations where I use my primary PSP, but the secondary PSP breaks through?

Below are the ingredients that make up situationality—but the recipe is different every time. At times, one or more of the factors will have a greater impact on your PSP approach. Building your awareness or even keeping a decision journal—as I do for all big decisions—will help you better understand how the different situational factors play out in different decisions. What happens to your decision-making and PSP approach when you are at work versus at home? When you are the expert versus the trainee? When you are deciding with family versus coworkers? When you are deciding about taking a vacation you've always dreamed about versus whether or not to replace some old pipes? Understanding the delicate interplay of situational factors can lead you to achieve a more ideal decision-making approach.

Use this activity to assess the interplay of situational factors that impact decision-making so that you can achieve a more ideal decision-making approach.

In any (decision-making) scene there are four factors you want to tease out: place, life stage, people, and decision ownership.

1. **Place:** both the physical space and the context. Are you in a classroom as the teacher or the student? Do you have the corner office, or are you working in a shared space with others on your team? Or are you working from home, at the desk in your bedroom while your two-year-old is napping? Are you working in a new space, or one you've been working in for years?

2. **Life stage:** Are you a teenager or a retiree? Starting a career, at the peak, or counting the days until retirement? If you've been in the same position for a while, is the job changing around you, or are you following the same protocols and procedures you've been following for years?

3. **People:** Who are the other stakeholders and what is their relationship to you? If you're a teacher deciding to move a test date, you have control of that decision, but you want the students to be adequately prepared. If you're the student, you may have information the teacher doesn't have—such as other tests being given in other classes—and moving a test date affects you and your future.

4. **Decision ownership:** How much will you (or your organization) be impacted by the decision outcome? And how important is the decision to you (or your organization)? Note that impact and importance are not the same thing. Impact is about having an effect on someone or something; importance is about significance or value. A given decision can have a significant impact but be of little importance, or vice versa. And it can be of differing importance to different people involved in the decision. If you are a teacher deciding when to schedule a quiz, for example, your decision may be of great importance to you because how the students perform on the quiz will drive your lesson planning. At the same time, it may have little impact on the students if the quizzes only count for 10 percent of their grade.

I asked these questions of Miriam to help her decide how to approach her relationship with an important coworker, and below are her responses.

COMPLETED CHEETAH SHEET 14
Situationality. Miriam's Example

CEO Miriam, a Listener, used this activity to assess the interplay of situational factors impacting her decision-making with her coworker Andre to achieve a more ideal decision-making approach.

1. Place: Where are you physically and the context?
   Working remotely on my business.

2. Life stage: What's your life stage? What's the life stage of the stakeholder?
   I'm a founder and CEO of a start-up company. It's my first time in these positions. I'm in my thirties. Andre is an employee in his thirties and this is his first start-up. We work remotely.

3. People: Who are the other stakeholders and what is their relationship to you?
   Andre is my second in command and we have been working together for about a year.

4. Decision ownership:
   a. How much will you (or your organization) be impacted by the decision outcome?
   A lot because this relationship is important to my business success.

   b. And how important is the decision to you (or your organization)?
   Extremely important. I just split with my cofounder and cannot afford to lose Andre.

Miriam had already seen one work relationship blow up, and it nearly took her start-up down with it. When she had initially completed the PSP module, Miriam identified herself as a Listener. However, in the business relationship that went south, Miriam could see that part of the problem was that her Listener self hadn't been listening. Instead, she'd been listening to her Adventurer self, assuming that her second-in-command didn't need connection and communication because she didn't. She realized that she is good at listening to new ideas and new people, but not so good at nurturing existing relationships—both professional and personal.

Below is the Cheetah Sheet for identifying your Secondary PSP followed by the one that Miriam completed to identify hers. To uncover herself as an Adventurer, she put aside "Work Miriam" and focused on "Relationship Miriam."

What is your secondary PSP?

CHEETAH SHEET 15
Secondary PSP

Use this activity to ferret out other decision approach tendencies that may be influenced by both prior experience and the situation you find yourself in. Note you'll want to reference Cheetah Sheet 14 when completing this activity.

Begin by assessing situationality. Use it as your "intake" form.

1. What situations did you imagine when you completed your primary PSP self-assessment?
2. Think of a situation that is very different from the situation you placed yourself in the PSP module.
   a. For example, if you thought about how you make decisions at work, think of how you make decisions with your family life.
3. Now take the PSP quiz again placing yourself in that different situation.
4. What is your PSP result?
5. Reflect on the following questions:
   a. What are the situations in which your primary PSP is in charge?
   b. What are the situations in which your secondary PSP is in charge?
   c. What are the situations where they complement each other?
   d. What are the situations when they are in conflict?

COMPLETED CHEETAH SHEET 15
Secondary PSP. Miriam's Example

Miriam, a Listener, is the chief executive of a start-up company. She struggles with personal relationships but is dismissive of that; however, after a work relationship failed and nearly took her start-up down with it, Miriam suspects that there is another PSP at play (and at work). Knowing that Listeners tend to have strong re-lationships—which she does not—she decides to use this activity to ferret out other decision approach tendencies that might be interfering with her dominant PSP.

Begin by assessing situationality. Use it as your "intake" form.

1. What situations did you imagine when you completed your primary PSP self-assessment?
   I had imagined myself in new situations, where I want to present my best self.

2. Think of a situation that is very different from the situation you placed yourself in the PSP module.
   a. For example, if you thought about how you make decisions at work, think of how you make decisions with your family life.
   I focused on long-term relationships instead of new situations.

3. Now take the PSP quiz again placing yourself in that different situation.

4. What is your PSP result?
   I am an Adventurer!

5. Reflect on the following questions:
   a. What are the situations in which your primary PSP is in charge?
      I make decisions as a Listener when I am in new situations.
   b. What are the situations in which your secondary PSP is in charge?
      In long-term relationships and in situations where a work decision needs to be made, my Adventurer becomes my dominant PSP. I like making new friendships—it's exciting—but I often feel that taking the time to maintain those friendships feels inefficient, a waste of my time. I've created a false equation between efficiency and efficacy. Of course, friendship is not a one-time event; friendships need time and attention. And of course I need to listen to my coworker and give our relationship time and attention.
   c. What are the situations where they complement each other?
      I am good at making friends and being dynamic, which are useful to someone who wants to create a start-up.
   d. What are the situations when they are in conflict?
      My Adventurer self prevents me from really thinking about other peoples' perspectives. Creating a start-up requires more than one person; I need to see my coworker Andre more like a friend than an underling.

Miriam learned that when it comes to her interpersonal behavior, she's an Adventurer. As an Adventurer, Miriam liked to make decisions quickly and assertively. She enjoyed the thrill of the new—new friends, new ideas, new situations—which meant she didn't tend to the garden of "old"—old friends, old ideas, old (comfortable) situations.

Miriam could immediately see the truth—and the problem—of being an Adventurer. "Once I make a friend," Miriam observed, "I think I have a friend. I think to myself that I don't need to keep making that friendship over and over." But Miriam's friends felt differently. And so did her coworker, Andre.

Now that you have stepped back from your decision-making to think about both situationality and your secondary PSP, it's time to apply this knowledge to the particular decision that you are struggling with or unhappy about. Ask yourself these clarifying questions, which I have organized into a Cheetah Sheet.

CHEETAH SHEET 16
Discerning Your Situationality

Use this activity to apply your knowledge of situationality and your secondary PSP to a decision. Note you'll want to reference Cheetah Sheet 14: Situationality and Cheetah Sheet 15: Secondary PSP when completing this activity.

Answer the questions below to place yourself in your specific decision-making story, and imagine a different ending.

1. What is the decision being made?

2. What is your PSP in this situation?

3. How would you historically have made this decision?

4. What is uncomfortable about that pattern in this situation?

5. Looking at the four ingredients of situationality (place, life stage, people, and decision ownership), which one or two are most important to you in this situation?

6. Think of yourself as a character in this story. What could your character do to achieve a successful outcome for this decision?

7. Identify one or two concrete steps that you could take that move you toward a more satisfying and successful outcome.

Miriam, a Listener, is the chief executive of a start-up company. She struggles with relationships. To better examine this issue and a key relationship with her coworker, Andre, she uses Cheetah Sheet 15: Discerning Your Situationality to ferret out other decision approach tendencies that may be influenced by her prior experience and the situation she finds herself in.

1. What is the decision being made?
   How can I improve my relationship with an important coworker, Andre?

2. What is your PSP in this situation?
   I am an Adventurer.

3. How would you historically have made this decision?
   I would have focused on how exciting the work is and ignored the relationship because the work is what matters most to me.

4. What is uncomfortable about that pattern in this situation?
   I am worried about losing Andre, which will hurt my ability to do the work that I am excited about.

5. Looking at the four ingredients of situationality, which one or two are most important to you in this situation?
   Decision ownership: I realize that the onus is on me to build a better and more effective relationship.

6. Think of yourself as a character in this story. What could your character do to achieve a successful outcome for this decision?
   What feels natural to me is not effective for others and does not work. Since giving time to a relationship doesn't feel natural, I need a model. The very person with whom I want to better relate—Andre—could be the model. I've always admired how quickly and effectively he replies to emails and how thoroughly and completely he finishes his assignments.

7. Identify one or two concrete steps that you could take that move you toward a more satisfying and successful outcome.
   a. **I will let Andre know how much I appreciate the way he communicates with me.**
   b. **I will ask him to suggest specific, concrete actions I can take to strengthen our work relationship, write down his answers, and commit to doing those things each week.**

Miriam did not relish spending more time in what she called "relationship-land"; it felt uncomfortable and unnecessary to her. But she realized that what worked for her didn't work for the people in her personal life—and the people in her start-up. Further, as the CEO and decision owner she needed to see—and take on—her leadership role more holistically. The ability to control meeting agendas and conversations was hers, but it wasn't working for her to expect others to be satisfied with her lack of connection and communication.

When Miriam took the time to focus on her relationship with Andre, even though it didn't feel comfortable or natural, she received tremendous positive reinforcement. Taking the risk reined in her Adventurer and allowed her to feel the satisfaction that a Listener gets from connectivity. More importantly, it challenged the story she'd been telling herself—that she was "bad" at relationships and there was nothing she could do about it. By committing to this small—but hard—change, Miriam felt more optimistic about herself and her start-up, and more in control of her future.

Even someone as Visionary as Ari can benefit from thinking about the situationality and variability of their decision-making tendencies. Recently, after some months of working together, I asked Ari to retake the PSP module to learn about his secondary PSP. His finding? Ari is secondarily a Thinker. He was so excited. "It feels amazing, like I'm a new person. I'm in position now to get closer to succeeding at the level I want to operate at, and to be doing a better job for Protect Her Life. I had it in me and I was able to change, for the better."

How did he do it? Ari says, "Since learning that I'm a Visionary, I started to see the downside to heuristics and to making decisions as a Visionary. Leaning into my Visionary thinking was leading to negative effects on my decision-making and on how I run Protect Her Life. Naming how I operated, and building self-awareness and language for what it means, has made me intentionally check and challenge myself, and I've deliberately been trying to adjust."

After we discussed situationality, I asked Ari what specific steps he wanted to take. He said, "I've done two primary things: I am trying to identify when, in a meeting or work setting, I take a conversation off in a tangent from the main point because sometimes I can lean into my creativity too much." Ari laughed ruefully. "I've also learned that it's okay to ask someone else in the meeting what the conversation topic is supposed to be. I can get so far off track in my own head.

"Second, by observing my own reactions and trying to be more patient, I'm aiming not to react to my ideas immediately. I can see that I benefit by allowing time to just (Cheetah) pause."

As a Visionary, Ari loves big, bold, new ideas. But too many new ideas—and new actions—is counterproductive and even harmful for Protect Her Life. In focusing on situationality, Ari says he is noticing that "I'm building a clear capacity to say 'no' more effectively so I don't stray from what's most important."

The world can seem random and unpredictable, while our own actions and reactions can seem automatic. But the world is often less random than we believe, and we can exercise more intentionality over our behavior than we often do.

Creating the world we want to live in, the relationships we want to share, and the environments we want to belong to takes skill-building, awareness, and careful practice. But slowing down long enough to learn about our decision-making patterns and habits can make us feel like we better understand what drives us and makes us unique. It can give us tools to have more agency while making others feel heard and valued.

Twenty-four centuries ago, Democritus suggested that everything was made of building blocks called atoms. He imagined a world in which a relatively small number of atoms—twenty or so—made up all matter: "It is possible for them to combine in diverse modes, in order to produce comedies or tragedies, ridiculous stories or epic poems." Although he was somewhat off in the number of atoms—there are currently 118 elements in the periodic table—he was right that they are the building blocks of our world. And they don't exist alone: they are usually in relationship with other atoms.

We, like atoms, rarely exist alone. We move through the world in combination with other people, places, and situations. We need to better see the building blocks of each situation we face. Like Tim, Miriam, and Ari we have the tools and the ability to grow into being better dynamic decision makers.

Chapter Fifteen

The Relationship between PSPs and Life Outlook

In all human affairs there are efforts, and there are results, and the strength of the effort is the measure of the result.
—James Allen, *As a Man Thinketh*

As I was finishing writing this book, Ari told me about eleven-year-old Chhaya. Her parents had died and she was being raised by her aunt. One day, her aunt told her to pack a suitcase: they were going on an overnight trip. Chhaya didn't know where they were going, but her aunt had bought her unusual pajamas, skimpy and silky and not at all familiar or comfortable. When they arrived in Ahmedabad, a strange man met them at the train station. Chhaya stood nervously to one side as the aunt and the man spoke. Then, suddenly, the police appeared and in an instant both the man and her aunt were taken away. Chhaya felt alone and frightened.

But Protect Her Life was there too. Someone in their intelligence network had previously identified the man and was watching him, knowing that he was going to meet a woman who had agreed to sell her niece.

The aunt was arrested and put in jail, where she is awaiting trial. Chhaya is living in a shelter, where she will now have the chance to continue her childhood. The best part of this story is that Chhaya didn't have to be rescued *after* she had been sold into a life of prostitution; she was saved before the crime was committed—and before her childhood was stolen.

In the year that I've worked with Ari, Tim, and Protect Her Life, their willingness to explore their PSPs, both strengths and weaknesses, and their open embrace of situationality and dynamic decision-making have transformed the nonprofit into a focused, team-oriented, effective organization.

Ari and Tim transformed from idealistic cofounders who wanted to address all aspects of sex trafficking in Ahmedabad to insightful leaders who have focused on one clear (ambitious) goal: to disrupt criminal networks by identifying, arresting, and convicting linchpin criminals in sex-trafficking organizations. Because the organization drilled down on their goals and began to operate in a more purposeful, cooperative, and streamlined manner, they have been able to do something they hadn't even dreamt about: preventing those criminals from committing the crimes that would have gotten them arrested.

Two Visionary leaders have become practical and process-oriented in figuring out how to think through and communicate their vision in a way they never could have envisioned. They started their journey looking outward, but in order to work effectively "out there," they had to learn to look inward. They could never have accomplished so much without that important step. The hard work of their charity's success began with self-reflection and study.

Sitting in stillness was neither easy nor natural for Ari and Tim—as it is not easy or natural for most of us—but it's what enabled them to achieve the amazing outcomes that are taking place now.

They never let go of their Visionary cores, but they were able to limit the blind spots and biases by leaning into behaviors that might be natural for other decision makers but were not natural for them. Once they drilled down on their values and what they really wanted to accomplish with their Vision of Success, they took their time to derive their Critical Concepts, and then, instead of deciding that the vision was the plan, they took time to collect data, speak with others, compare what they'd learned, and challenge their assumptions and judgments, all of which enabled them to still be Visionaries—but Visionaries with an evidence-based, practical, and actionable plan.

Like Ari and Tim, each of us has a life outlook that comes from our decision-making approach. After all, our decisions make our lives. For Ari and Tim, the idea of tackling a monster problem wasn't off-putting. It might be to you or to me, but something so ambitious is part of the Visionary makeup.

Each PSP has a life outlook that stems from their decision-making approach—and each one has a certain beauty to it. The Adventurer is oriented toward forward movement; the future is always more interesting than the present. The Detective is oriented to drill down and dig for information because the world is an endlessly absorbing place. The Listener is oriented toward asking questions because other people and their experiences give contour and color to the world. The Thinker is oriented toward thinking deeply: the engrossing action happens between their ears. And as for the Visionary, they are looking for rainbows no one else has seen, but when the rest of us can catch a glimpse, boy, is it something to behold.

Ari and Tim never changed their basic life outlook; they remain true Visionaries. This will be true for all of us; we are who we are, at some level. But by taking the time to understand ourselves, our outlook on life, and how we move in the world, we can become better versions of ourselves—and build better versions of our relationships.

The great Zen Buddhist teacher Thich Nhat Hanh, talking about mastering the art of being with others, once observed that "if you pour a handful of salt into a cup of water, the water becomes undrinkable. But if you pour the salt into a river, people can continue to draw the water to cook, wash, and drink. The river is immense, and it has the capacity to receive, embrace, and transform."[1] Many of us think that we exist in a cup, and we make decisions as though that is true—"it's my decision alone, and only I know how to make it." Living this way leads us to poison the water in our self-created cups.

We have the option to move through the world seeing ourselves as part of a river: on our own decision-making journey, certainly, but bumping up against others who shape and impact the direction of that journey, and whose journey we shape and impact. If we can be more mindful both about our own decision-making and the decision-making strengths and biases of others in the river, we can cocreate a more productive, impactful, and satisfying life for ourselves and for those around us.

Glossary

Ambiguous situations Those situations where the best outcome is a matter of interpretation.

Analysis paralysis Inability to make a decision due to overthinking a problem.

AREA Method A perspective-taking decision-making system that uniquely controls for and counters cognitive biases by understanding the incentives and motives of others so that you expand your knowledge while improving your judgement. AREA is an acronym that gets its name from the perspectives that it addresses: Absolute, Relative, Exploration & Exploitation, and Analysis.

Authority bias The tendency to give more weight than perhaps you should to the opinions of those with structural power.

Behavior questions Questions that address what someone does or has done.

Cheetah pause Cheetah Pauses are strategic stops that temporarily slow you down to speed up your efficacy. They are named after the cheetah and its ability to decelerate quickly, making it an agile and flexible hunter.

Closeness-communication bias Overestimating the effectiveness of your communication when engaging with someone you consider close, whether it's a romantic partner, a friend, or a colleague.

Cognitive biases Systematic errors and mental mistakes in thinking that occur when people process and interpret information in the world around them, impacting their decisions and judgments.

Community A social unit in which there is some commonality, such as norms, religion, values, customs, geography, or identity.

Confirmation bias The tendency to interpret new evidence as confirmation of one's existing beliefs or theories.

Contextual data Constricts our thinking and leads to a framing bias: The context in which we receive the data impacts how we think about it.

Critical Concepts Derived from a Vision of Success, these are the researchable questions you need to solve for and the concrete actions you will take to move from where you are to achieving your Vision of Success.

Data traps Ways that data may lead us astray and be misinterpreted based on cognitive biases.

Dynamic decision maker   Your ability to inhabit other PSPs to account for your situationality.

Feeling questions   Questions that address how someone responds emotionally to a topic.

Frame blindness   The tendency to miss the bigger picture, leading to problems such as solving the wrong problem or only part of the problem that you are grappling with.

Inversion   Solving a problem by starting at the end. Rather than first focusing on the problem itself, the problem solver begins by determining their success metrics. To do that the problem solver crafts a Vision of Success and then derives Critical Concepts, the few factors that need to be deeply and creatively investigated to attain the success metric.

Knowledge questions   Explore what factual information the respondent has about your topic.

Lexicon   The vocabulary that you use to communicate your thoughts and feelings.

Life stage   Where you are in your life in terms of age, experience level, place, and community.

Liking bias   The tendency to overlook the faults of, and comply with, wishes of well-liked others.

Loss aversion   The tendency to prefer avoiding losses to acquiring equivalent gains.

Narrative bias   The tendency to overvalue story lines and undervalue data.

Opinion questions   Tackle what someone thinks about a topic, action, or event.

Optimism bias   A belief that things are likely to go our way.

Patterned data   Prompts the *clustering illusion*—also known in sports and gambling as the "hot hand fallacy"—whereby we assume that random events are information that will help us predict a future event.

Planning fallacy   A prediction phenomenon, all too familiar to many, wherein people underestimate the time it will take to complete a future task, despite knowledge that previous tasks have generally taken longer than planned.

Problem Solver Profile   A personal approach to decision-making that incorporates strengths and blind spots derived from specific cognitive biases that reveal patterns of behavior that drive decision-making.

    Adventurer   Values gut reactions.

    Detective   Values following the data.

    Listener   Values soliciting the input of others.

    Thinker   Values identifying multiple paths and outcomes.

    Visionary   Values seeing paths others don't.

Projection bias   A feature in human thinking where one thinks that others have the same priority, attitude, or belief that one harbors oneself, even if this is unlikely to be the case.

Relativity bias   Keeps you from seeing things as they actually are and inclines you to see them in comparison to something else.

Risk analysis   The process of identifying, estimating, and assessing factors that could negatively affect a person, place, or thing.

Risk appetite   The level of exposure you (or your organization) are willing to take.

Risk assessment   Defining criteria to gauge if a decision is within your risk threshold.

Saliency bias   Getting attached to the most recent or bold information or ideas, even if they aren't ultimately the most important.

Salient data   When we overweight new or noteworthy information, resulting in suboptimal decision-making, planning errors, and more.

Scarcity bias   The tendency to overvalue originality because it's rare.

Situationality   The time, place, and people around you when you are making a decision. To determine your situationality, consider that in any (decision-making) scene there are four factors you want to tease out: place; life stage; people; and decision ownership.

Social proof bias   The tendency to be swayed to do what others recommend, instead of thinking about what you actually want.

Vision of Success   Part of the AREA Method decision-making system that uses inversion to help you identify your decision's success metrics. It answers the question: What has to happen in the outcome of my decision for me to know that it has succeeded for me or my organization? It helps you get clear on why you are solving your problem and what your desired outcome is, and it helps you derive your **Critical Concepts**, those few factors you need to investigate and understand to solve for your success.

Notes

Acknowledgments

1. James Baldwin, *Nothing Personal* (Boston: Beacon Press, 2021), 50.
2. Hannah Arendt, *The Human Condition*, 2nd ed. (University of Chicago Press, 1958), 190.
3. Nicky Gumbel, Twitter post, March 9, 2018, 12:02 p.m. https://twitter.com/nickygumbel/status/972155585910190080.

Chapter One.   How Do You Decide?

Epigraph: Marianne Williamson, *A Course In Weight Loss: 21 Spiritual Lessons for Surrendering Your Weight Forever* (Carlsbad, CA: Hay House, 2012), 158.

Chapter Five.   The Listener

Epigraph: quoted in Janet Lowe, *Oprah Winfrey Speaks: Insights from the World's Most Influential Voice* (New York: John Wiley & Sons, 1998), 20.
1. "Oprah Talks to Nelson Mandela," Oprah.com, accessed June 26, 2022, https://www.oprah.com/world/oprah-interviews-nelson-mandela/7.

Chapter Six.   The Thinker

1. MIA Mass Meeting at Holt Street Baptist Church, December 5, 1955, Martin Luther King, Jr. Research and Education Institute, https://kinginstitute.stanford.edu/king-papers/documents/mia-mass-meeting-holt-street-baptist-church.

Chapter Seven.   The Visionary

Epigraph: Steve Jobs, "Secrets of Life," interview with Santa Clara Valley Historical Society, 1994, available on YouTube, https://www.youtube.com/watch?v=kYfNvmF0Bqw.
1. "Beyoncé's Evolution," *Harper's Bazaar*, August 10, 2021, https://www.harpersbazaar.com/culture/features/a37039502/beyonce-evolution-interview-2021.
2. Quoted in John Sculley and John A. Byrne, *Odyssey: Pepsi to Apple: A Journey of Adventure, Ideas, and the Future* (New York: Harper Collins, 1987).

Chapter Eight.   Hunt Like the Cheetah

Epigraph: W. Edwards Deming, *The Essential Deming: Leadership Principles from the Father of Quality*, ed. Joyce Nilsson Orsini (New York: McGraw Hill, 2013), 79.

Chapter Nine.   PSPs and Risk Profiles

Epigraph: Naved Abdali, *Investing Hopes, Hypes, and Heartbreaks: The Game Is Rigged and Is Rigged in Your Favor* (Mississauga, ON: Rosehurst Publishing, 2021), 123.

Chapter Eleven.   Ambiguity versus Uncertainty

Epigraph: Elvis Presley quoted in Adam Victor, *The Elvis Encyclopedia* (New York: Overlook Duckworth, 2008), 428.

Chapter Thirteen.   How PSPs Color Our Relationship with Data

Epigraph: Albert Einstein, Address to Prussian Academy of Sciences, 1921.

Chapter Fourteen.   Situationality and Dynamic Decision-Making

Epigraph: Gurudev Sri Sri Ravi Shankar (@SriSri), Twitter, February 17, 2018, https://twitter.com/srisri/status/964912883401416705?lang=en.

Chapter Fifteen.   The Relationship between PSPs and Life Outlook

1. Thich Nhat Hanh, *How to Love* (Berkeley, CA: Parallax Press, 2015).

Cast of Problem Solvers (in Order of Appearance)

Ari: Founder of Protect Her Life, a nonprofit organization dedicated to the mission of giving freedom to children and women from sex trafficking. [*Visionary*]

Tim: Co-founder of Protect Her Life with Ari. [*Visionary*]

Andrew: Chief executive and cofounder of a national nonprofit in high schools called the Future Project. [*Visionary*]

Ruth: Taught her husband more about her love language (words of affirmation) through developing a shared lexicon. [*Listener*]

Sam: The dutiful husband who moved a purse for his wife, finally understood after developing a shared lexicon. [*Thinker*]

Baba: A senior accountant at a top international accounting firm who changed careers and attended graduate school on a whim. [*Adventurer*]

Doris: Mother (of Sharon) who was unable to hold her tongue when talking to her daughter's ex-husband. [*Adventurer*]

Sharon: Daughter (of Doris) who had asked that her mother not talk to her ex-husband during an extended family event. [*Detective*]

Aanya: A physician who focused primarily on research and was asked to draft a letter responding to an unexpected fatality. [*Detective*]

Flor: A mid-level technology executive, responsible for coordinating across departments and vendors. Worked closely with Randi. [*Listener*]

Randi: A project manager for a software company. Worked closely with Flor. [*Detective*]

Linda: Neighborhood association member who was part of the "walking" disagreement and reached out to Irwin. [*Listener*]

Irwin: An older neighborhood association member who was furious about walkers being too far out in the street. [*Adventurer*]

Michael: CEO of a mental wellness start-up facing multiple urgent decisions. [*Thinker*]

Olga: A stock analyst who thrived when comparing different financial outcomes. [*Thinker*]

Jason: Employee at a consulting company where he has the opportunity to work with new clients every couple of weeks. [*Visionary*]

Niko: Captain of a luxury cruise ship who explored his PSP by conducting a rear-view exercise about a previous work decision involving lobsters. [*Detective*]

Lisa: Divorced woman newly on dating apps who talked through her problems with Rhianna and Stephanie. [*Detective*]

Rhianna: Gives Lisa advice on the context of her dating life. [*Thinker*]

Stephanie: Gives Lisa advice on the optics of her dating life. [*Adventurer*]

Tony: A senior manager navigating whether or not to cancel an upcoming conference. [*Thinker*]

Saadia: A professional writer who was approached by Kavita to work on a project together. [*Detective*]

Kavita: Launching a new project to support women with leadership coaching. Working with Saadia. [*Visionary*]

Calvin: A junior designer at a well-established, brand-name global company. Works with Talia. [*Listener*]

Talia: Calvin's supervisor, who gives Calvin feedback on his work in a direct and focused way. [*Thinker*]

Avonelle: A daughter and sister who wants to figure out a family get-together during the COVID-19 pandemic. [*Detective*]

Clara: Instructional coach working with Sam. [*Listener*]

Sam: Young science teacher being coached by Clara. [*Visionary*]

Eric: Founder of Peace First. [*Visionary*]

John: Founder of a basic health care charity called the Oda Foundation in rural Nepal. His high-stakes decision is chronicled in Cheryl's first book, *Problem Solved: A Powerful System for Making Complex Decisions with Confidence and Conviction.* [*Thinker*]

Miriam: Chief executive and founder of an agriculture technology start-up company. [*Listener*]

Andre: Miriam's employee. [*Listener*]

Index

Abdali, Naved, 67

Absolute perspective, in AREA Method, 12, 13, 153

accountability: Protect Her Life and, 127–28; Thinker PSP and focus on, 92

adolescents, decision-making program for, 15–16, 53–54

Adventurer PSP, 8, 27–33, 154; blind spots of, xix, 27–28, 60, 84, 87; closeness-communication bias of, 28, 31–32, 84; confirmation bias of, 28, 84; and data, relationship with, 124, 125; and Detective PSP, cognitive biases in relationship of, 93, 112–13; examples of, 9, 28–33; life outlook of, 150–51; optimism bias of, 28, 29, 30, 33, 82, 84, 87; planning fallacy of, 28, 29, 84, 93; risk profile of, 70, 71, 72, 73; as secondary PSP, 136, 144–45; situationality and use of, 138; strengths of, xix, 27, 60, 84, 87; tips for, 31; Visionary PSP compared to, 54–55, 90

Ahmedabad, India, 5; children sold into sex slavery in, 5–6. *See also* Protect Her Life

Allen, James, 149

ambiguity/ambiguous situations, 100–101, 153; vs. uncertainty, 100; values and path through, 102, 103

Amundsen, Roald, 32

Analysis, in AREA Method, 12, 153

analysis paralysis, 153; Thinker PSP and, 45, 46; tips for avoiding, 48

app(s): dating, decision-making regarding, 69–70; Problem Solver Profile (PSP), 8, 15–16

AREA Method, 11–14, 153; adapting to high-school students, 15–16, 53–54;

applications of, 13; evaluation of, 14; Google compared to, 12–13; inversion used by, 101, 155; origins of, 11–12, 120; as perspective-taking system, 12, 120; and Problem Solver Profiles (PSPs), 15–16; questions used in, 129; website for, 4

Arendt, Hannah, xvii

Ari (pseudonym). *See* Patel, Ari

Aristotle, 3

assumptions: checking and challenging, 4, 11, 12, 14, 24–25, 65, 95, 97, 116, 120, 131–32, 150; about data, 121–22, 123; Detective PSP and, 89, 90; differences in decision-making styles and, 23, 25; and faulty decision-making, 61–62, 89–90; inner voice colored by, xvii; about other stakeholders' motivations, 115, 117; values and, 108, 116

authority bias, 153; Listener PSP and, 40, 84; Thinker PSP and, 45, 85, 92

Bad Feminist (Gay), 33

Baldwin, James, xvii

Barron's (magazine), 11

"bearish" company story, 11–12

behavior questions, 129, 132, 153

Beyoncé, 56

blind spots: of Adventurer PSP, xix, 27–28, 60, 84, 87; Cheetah Sheet for, 84–85; of Detective PSP, xix, 35, 60, 84, 87; of Listener PSP, xix, 39–40, 60, 84, 87, 91; reframing as strengths, in relationships, 97–98, 109, 110–17; of Thinker PSP, xix, 45, 60, 85, 87; use of term, 59; of Visionary PSP, xix, 8, 51–52, 60, 69, 81–82, 85, 87. *See also* cognitive biases

Printed in the USA
CPSIA information can be obtained
at www.ICGtesting.com
CBHW080002190324
5549CB00011B/474

9 781501 768033